Football
Fireworks for a
Hot Fourth
Short Sacred Rite of
Search and Destruction

Three plays by Jon Swan

Grove Press, Inc.
New York

CONTENTS

Football
a one-act play

This play was first performed at the Seattle Repertory Theatre's Off Center Theatre, Seattle, Washington, on November 14, 1968. It was one of a group of one-act plays by Jon Swan, *Three Cheers for Whats-Its-Name*, which were directed by Josef Sommer. Scenery was designed by Peter Horne and costumes were designed by Jack Smith. The cast was as follows:

GORE	Jason Bernard
NORDEN	Bernard Frawley
GEIGER	Stanley Anderson
CLAYMORE	John Odegard
THE COACH	Robert Loper
MRS. ASHLAND	Maureen Quinn

CHARACTERS

COACH
CLAYMORE
NORDEN
GEIGER   } *four male reporters*
GORE
MRS. ASHLAND, *a female reporter*

*The stage is an abstract of a football locker room. Down-
stage center, a bench stands in front of a tall red locker
numbered, in white, 1. Longer-legged than most locker
room benches, this one is about two feet tall. To the right
of the bench, five football helmets with face-cages are
lined up, evenly spaced, on the floor; five others, to the left.
Behind these helmets, in two rows on either side of the
locker but farther upstage, hang ten soiled football uniforms—shoulder-braced and padded tops and stiff, tough
bottoms. They hang, from their long invisible wires, stoutly
rather than limply. The bottoms of the bottoms come
down to about top-of-the-locker level. Two motionless
tackle-dummies also hang, one on each side of the stage.
Upstage left, five red megaphones stand in a row, big-
mouth down. At the start, the stage is rather dimly lit
except for the bright patch by the bench above which a
green-shaded light bulb hangs.*

When the curtain opens, the COACH—*a figure made
colossal by his football uniform—is seen sitting on the
bench. His uniform may be three sizes too large for him,
but it is stuffed to the bursting point. The cleats on his
enormous football shoes are doubly long. Perched above*

his swollen outfit, the Coach's head emerges incongruously puny. He wears no helmet—it rests beside him on the bench and is, like the locker, numbered 1—but does wear glasses. His hair is thin; he may be bald. He is in his mid-fifties.

The COACH *faces dead ahead, hands on his knees, with an expression of grim but benevolent determination. He holds this pose for a time, then—slowly at first and then quickly—glances off right, raises his head in inquiry, then, surprised, switches his face back front just as a suave formal baritone makes an announcement over a microphone.*

BARITONE: Ladies and gentlemen, our coach.

COACH (*briskly picking up on the introduction*): Who's ready if you are, ladies and gentlemen. Good evening.

CHORUS OF REPORTERS (*bobbing up from their seats in the theater*): Good evening, coach!

COACH: Well, all I can say is, I hope you fellows are in training because . . . (*In a confidential tone.*) Hear I'm in for a rough one. (*Then briskly again.*) Now. First in ten and a long way to go . . .

A flurry of hands shoots up in the audience. The COACH *abruptly abandons his joshing face, assuming a patient, paternal, earnestly attentive expression.*

Yes, Mr. Claymore.

CLAYMORE (*rising*): Sir, apropos . . .

COACH: Little bit louder, please, Mr. Claymore, and you might skip the French while you're at it.

CLAYMORE (*in a louder but deeper voice*): Sir, in all due relevance to your pre-game pep, I wonder if we might safely conclude that the flickering light at the end of the tunnel has taken a turn for the better and, having turned the corner and broken the back, we've come to the crux so to speak?

COACH: What crux?

CLAYMORE: I'm afraid I don't know, sir. You left the matter up in the air.

COACH: You mean, Mr. Claymore, did he actually catch the pass?

CLAYMORE: Yes, sir. That's just what I mean. (*He sits down.*)

COACH: He definitely caught the . . . Mr. Claymore, so far as I know there has never been the slightest question about his catching that pass. You know Keith. That boy has a hand like a bucket and fingers of glue. He's the kind couldn't fumble a greased pig in a snowstorm. Why, he . . . (*pulling himself up short*). The only question that *has* been raised—and raised, mind you, by the usual elements—is whether the ball was, on receival, still regulation size.

CLAYMORE *pops back up.*

CLAYMORE: Was it?

COACH (*fluently*): At this juncture, at this point in the game, all I can say is that on-the-spot photos made on the spot are still being duly processed. (*Recognizing another hand.*) Yes, Mr. Norden.

NORDEN *rises as* CLAYMORE *sits.*

NORDEN: Good evening, sir.

COACH: Good evening, Norden.

NORDEN: Sir, a further question relating to . . .

COACH: Little bit louder, if you please, Mr. Norden.

NORDEN: Sir, a further question relating to . . . Can you hear me now, sir?

COACH: I can, Mr. Norden—loud and clear.

NORDEN: . . . relating to regulations other than those concerning the ball. The question raised is whether regulations were altered perhaps during the course of the game not only on their side but on our side as well.

COACH: Altered?

NORDEN: Either carelessly observed or completely altered. Yes, sir.

COACH: Under the stress of the moment, it is, of course, conceivable that a certain horseplay, a certain element of roughhouse sometimes develops but . . . Who did you say leveled these charges?

NORDEN: I didn't say, sir. But independent observers do claim . . .

COACH: Let me . . . let me . . . let me just ask you one thing, Mr. Norden. You mention these independent observers. Have you—I wonder—have you ever seen, at a football game, an *independent* observer? Why, the fans go crazy at a football game! Have you ever *been* to a football game?

NORDEN: I'm ashamed to confess, sir, I was too young for the last one.

COACH: I should think you would be, Norden. Next?

NORDEN *sits as another* REPORTER, *recognized, rises.*

REPORTER: Reports just in from the Bowl itself, sir, suggest that it may have been . . . (*halts in some trepidation*).

COACH: Yes?

REPORTER: May have been . . . (*halts again*).

COACH: Go ahead, Mister . . .

REPORTER: I was going to say, raining throughout the entire first quarter, sir.

COACH: Raining, Mr. Geiger?

GEIGER: Yes, sir, and that, be*cause* of this rain, those on-the-spot photographs scarcely show . . . scarcely provide . . .

COACH: You are aware, I suppose, of the official prediction for the weather on the day in question?

GEIGER: Sir, I am.

COACH: And what did they predicate—sun or rain?

GEIGER: They refused to go out on a limb, sir.

COACH: Be that as it may, our experts refused no such thing and there wasn't a single cloud in the sky. But now, even *if* weather of a nature such as the type you allude to *had* obtained, it would hardly provide hard proof of. Rain, Mr. Geiger, is a tricky thing. You are aware, I trust, of its effect on vision?

GEIGER: It makes observation more difficult?

COACH: Precisely. It brings down, as I understand it, it automatically interposes a kind of screen between the beholder and whatever it is he pretends to behold. So now your sources may say what they like but what I want to know is, how can you tell it's raining if you can't really see to see?

GEIGER: But the field was *muddy*, sir!

COACH: When, Mr. Geiger? When?

GEIGER: Right up to the half!

COACH: But we received samples of that ground in this morning's mail, Mr. Geiger, and that ground was perfectly dry!

CLAYMORE *rises fast and indignantly as* GEIGER *slumps back into his seat.*

CLAYMORE: Sir! I have—right here in my hand—a piece of that mud!

COACH (*smiling, relaxed*): I was sure you would, Mr. Claymore. You've earned your reputation, I see.

A woman reporter, recognized by a smile and a wave from the COACH, *rises as* CLAYMORE *sits.*

Yes, Mrs. Ashland. Your hands are clean, I trust, Mrs. Ashland.

MRS. ASHLAND: They certainly are this evening.

COACH: And what's on your mind, Mrs. Ashland?

MRS. ASHLAND (*plain and simple*): Sir, Keith caught the ball.

COACH: That's right. Keith caught the ball.

MRS. ASHLAND (*going a step further*): He caught the ball after a perfectly incredible run.

COACH (*quickly*): Incredible? You mean, Mrs. Ashland, you don't accept our . . .

MRS. ASHLAND: A perfectly *thrill*ing run from behind the forty-yard line all the way back to in back of their basket and caught it.

COACH: That's what he did. Yes.

MRS. ASHLAND: And the ball was regulation size when it left Kowalsky's hand?

COACH: It was indeed. In technical terms, the play was a successfully executed Statue-of-Liberty-fake-'em. It looks like a pass; they think it's a run; by the time the ball's in the air, they've had it.

MRS. ASHLAND: Yes. Well, what I wondered was how that ball could shrink all by itself in mid-air, sir.

COACH: Exactly our point! It couldn't! And therefore the touchdown was incontestably valid.

MRS. ASHLAND: But their photos show Keith hugging a ball the size of a golfball, sir!

COACH: Photos taken in a tropical downpour are hardly what we call proof, Mrs. Ashland!

GEIGER *and* NORDEN *rise swiftly.*

GEIGER: But sir!

NORDEN: How can you . . . ?

COACH (*firmly in command*): And, furthermore, the fact
. . . the fact that such weather obtains in the proof
they adduce, clearly, unmistakably, indicates that—
indicates only one thing: that their photos are either
touched-up, phony, or just plain staged. Staged. Taken
on a different day, in a different country far as that
goes, and using a different ball. You yourself, Mrs.
Ashland, described the ball as shown in their pictures
as a . . . ? Yes?

MRS. ASHLAND: Golfball.

GEIGER *and* NORDEN *sit.*

COACH: You see? But now, even supposing their documents
could be accepted as prime-face, supposing that pigskin *had* been deflated in the course of its incredible
journey—what alternative would we have other than
to pursue the course we are already pursuing? It would
mean only one thing and one thing only: that they
had interdicted our football with a needle-sharp missile
launched from a base which has subsequently been
completely demolished. They do things like that, what
choice do we have?

GEIGER *is back on his feet in an instant.* NORDEN,
slower, gets halfway up and then sits down. MRS. ASH-
LAND *is still standing.*

GEIGER: Then the football *wasn't* regulation at the time of
the touchdown?

COACH: I'd like to know just why the hell not!

GEIGER: Because it was hit! Punctured! Hit!

CLAYMORE *rises, one hand up.*

COACH: Can you prove that charge, Mr. Geiger? Will you kindly sit down, Mrs. Ashland? Who said it was snowing, Geiger? What do you want, Claymore? Oh boy, do I wish I could just meet you boys out on the . . . out on the field someday. (*In the course of his rage, he has picked up his helmet and crushed it flat in his hands. He looks at the helmet now as if wondering where it came from, then sets it down softly on the bench beside him. Then he rises.*) Out on the field . . . Yes, well. You know, you know, sometimes we get— it's only human, I guess—sometimes we all get a little worked up. At such times, an element of vituperation, an element of rancor makes itself evident in the course of our discourse—an element which, it seems to me, is completely inimical to the spirit of what I'd like to call here tonight Fair Play. I'd like us all—every least one of us—to look into our hearts and minds and check that tendency. Personally, personally, I feel that my contribution, *as* a coach, my own contribution to the youth of this country is nothing more or less, nothing humbler nor grander than to exercise that tendency while at the same time reining it in. My job, as I see it, is to inculcate in those young minds and vigorous developing bodies given unto my charge that sense of Fair Play—no matter how rough the physical contact of the game itself may, on occasion, be—that sense of Fair Play on which, it seems to me, our founding fathers both founded and fathered this country. A glance at our sister republics to the south shows us just what can, on occasion, result when this spirit has not been faithfully nurtured. Earlier in this century, the bickering lands of the Balkans provided yet another example of what happens to men who never learned to break it up when the whistle blows. History is, unfortunately, replete with examples. Caesar was a man who didn't know when to stop when the whistle of destiny had already blown—and Rome fell. Napoleon Bonaparte from the island of Corsica ignored the whistle not only once but time and again, and paid the penalty for so doing. Returned to the benches, he was henceforth forbidden the field—and ostracized. In our own epoch—in many ways the most modern epoch known to man—Adolf Hitler repeated the past, refused to play by the rules, and fell. A man can learn much, just by turning the pages of a history book. Each page has its story to tell. But a boy can learn too—on the basketball court, on the ice-hockey rink, out on the diamond, down in the crystal-clear waters of his high-school pool and last, but by no means least, out on the gridiron, out on the field, come fall, out on the field under the crisp skies of autumn as he fiercely pits both body and mind against his fellow-men, yet all in the spirit of good clean fun, in the spirit of what men, from time immemorial, have called, and I think rightly so—the spirit . . . the spirit of Fair Play.

The reporters applaud. The COACH, *misty-eyed and pleased, hushes them modestly with his broad flat hands.*

Now then, if I have been unduly brusque at times, if I have perhaps failed to keep my temper in check, if I have failed to heed the whistle within, I hope it will be forgiven me even as I, in the spirit of which I just spoke, forgive it you. (*He sits down again on his bench.*) Now, getting back to . . . back to the game— but cooled off, cooled down now, as I hope you are —let me just summarize by saying that *if* precautionary measures were taken, they were taken to obviate a situation which, had it occurred, would have endangered; (*his voice moves in a patient, weary chant-like rhythm now*) that those measures, *had* they been taken, would have been taken only after exhaustive; and, finally, that the size of the specific pigskin involved remains—as my good friend Mr. Claymore so well put it before—in the hands of our experts or— if you will—at least for the moment, still up in the air.

GORE *rises.* GORE—*dressed like a sporty Irishman or a bit like a well-dressed, in old clothes, race-track tout— is a short, lean, peppery man who speaks in a high-pitched, very clear, almost piercing, not quite British voice.*

Yes, Mr. Gore.

GORE: When is a cat not a cat?

The COACH, *still in his good-humored mood, responds with a good-humored working silence. The question puzzles him.*

I say, when is a cat not a cat?

COACH: I see. Yes. Just a . . . (*After a slight pause—hopefully.*) When it is a-sleep?

GORE: No, sir. When there are flies on its eyeballs and maggots in its mouth.

COACH (*still friendly, but troubled*): Why? What is it then?

GORE: It is dead, sir. (*He sits down as abruptly as he rose.*)

COACH: What are you driving at, Gore? What are you driving at? I . . . *we* didn't start to use razors first! *They* did, and you know that damn well!

GORE *shoots back up.*

GORE: Razors, sir?

COACH: Razors! Fixed to their shoes! Razors. One slice and there went your foot, all alone, still running, like a chicken with its head cut off!

NORDEN *rises.* GORE *remains standing.*

NORDEN (*heatedly*): You have documentary evidence of that?

COACH: I most certainly do. Here. In this box. (*He has picked up a shoebox from under his bench and now exhibits it.*)

NORDEN: There is a foot in that box?

COACH: There is.

NORDEN: The foot is a human foot?

COACH: The foot is a human foot, Norden.

NORDEN: And it was found on the field?

COACH: It most certainly was, Norden.

NORDEN: And is it one of ours or one of theirs?

COACH: What did you . . . ?

NORDEN: I say, is it one of ours or is it theirs?

COACH (*more quietly*): And just how would you tell the difference, Norden?

GORE *sits.*

NORDEN: By size and by color, sir.

COACH: I see.

NORDEN: By size and by color, by the trim of the nail, and by the calluses found on the sole, sir.

COACH: The calluses. Yes. You know, you're a shrewd man, Norden. Perhaps just a shade *too* shrewd. What—to spring one on you for a change—what size shoe do *you* wear, Norden?

NORDEN: I wear a size 12 shoe, sir.

COACH: Well, well. What a big foot you have, Mr. Norden. I shall take good care to send you a shoe that will, nevertheless, fit it nicely.

NORDEN: Just one shoe, sir?

COACH (*with cordial menace*): I think, Mr. Norden, just one will do. One step at a time, Mr. Norden.

MRS. ASHLAND, *recognized, rises slowly as* NORDEN *slowly sits.*

Yes, Mrs. Ashland.

MRS. ASHLAND: As I recall, sir . . .

COACH: Go ahead, Mrs. Ashland.

MRS. ASHLAND: As I recall sir, their use of . . . (*she halts again*).

COACH: Do go on, Mrs. Ashland.

MRS. ASHLAND: I no longer recall, sir. Thank you. Excuse me. I'm . . .

As MRS. ASHLAND *sits down, still speaking, in a state of alarm and confusion,* CLAYMORE *rises.*

CLAYMORE: As we recall, sir, their use of razors . . .

COACH (*cutting in*): Have you been recognized, Mr. Claymore?

CLAYMORE: Excuse me, sir. I have not.

CLAYMORE *sits down.* GEIGER *raises a hand.*

COACH: Yes, Mr. Geiger?

GEIGER (*rising*): As we recall, sir, their use of razors was in response to our use of cleats, some of which . . .

COACH: Cleats! What's wrong with cleats in a football game? You want us to play football in pumps? You ever kicked a sopping wet ball wearing pumps?

GEIGER: A ball wearing pumps, sir? Never.

COACH: Exactly!

GEIGER: But the cleats were sharp. They drove right through their shoes, right through their feet!

COACH: And why, Mr. Geiger? Because they showed up on the field wearing sneakers, that's why! Ever tried kicking a ball wearing sneakers?

GEIGER: Sir, I have.

COACH: Of course you have. Still, my theory is—and I think you'll agree—ask for trouble and that's what you'll get.

GEIGER: You think they were asking for it then, sir?

COACH: Well, that's certainly what they got, isn't it? You're not going to debate that, are you, Geiger?

GEIGER: No, sir. I won't.

> GEIGER *sits. The* COACH *checks a watch which isn't there.*

COACH: Well, that's that then, and now, ladies and gentlemen, I see our time's just about . . .

> GORE *rises abruptly, speaking as he rises.*

GORE: When is a porpoise not a porpoise?

COACH: Mr. Gore, I'm afraid . . .

GORE (*louder*): I say, when is a porpoise not a porpoise?

COACH: When . . . Wait a minute. I think I'm getting the hang of this . . . When it has lost its porpoise?

GORE: Precisely! And when is a dictator not a dictator?

COACH (*with growing enthusiasm*): When I say that he isn't?

GORE: Precisely!

> CLAYMORE, NORDEN, *and* ASHLAND *rise and call out in unison.*

THE THREE: And when is a war not a war?

COACH (*with the speed and joy of a born competitor*): When it is hell?

THE THREE: Precisely!

GEIGER *rises*.

GEIGER: And when is a Christian not a Christian?
COACH (*excited, exultant, rising*): I'm getting them all!
When he's a Christian *soldier*?
GEIGER: Precisely!

> *Colored spotlights rake and sweep the stage as the*
> COACH *springs into position for cheerleading and as*
> CLAYMORE, NORDEN, GEIGER, ASHLAND, *and* GORE—
> *adding their voices to his—rush to the stage, either*
> *leaping up onto it or springing up the stairs, left. They*
> *pick up megaphones and line up with the* COACH. *The*
> *chant-shout already underway is:*

ALL: *Chri*stian! *Sol*diers! Fight-fight-fight!
Hit 'em *left*! Hit 'em *right*!
Roll 'em *back* and move right *in*!
Christian soldiers, *win, win*, WIN!

> *The usual hand-rolling, fist-punching, back-arching,*
> *and choral leap, etc., accompany the above. When it*
> *is over, the* COACH *snatches a megaphone from a*
> *nearby reporter and booms an announcement out to*
> *the audience.*

COACH: Eeevereebody now! Let 'em hear it!

> *They go through the chant-shout rigamarole again.*
> *When it is completed, they look at each other, sud-*
> *denly quiet, as if hearing some strange sound. Putting*
> *their megaphones aside and their fingers to their lips,*
> *they all squat—their eyes fixed at some point off right.*
> *Then, very softly at first, then louder and louder:*

ALL: cchhhhhhhhhhHHHHHHHHHHH!!!

The sound, made in the throat and then moving up as if they were hawking a piece of phlegm, opens up tremendously at the end to sound, at last, like a jet taking off. As they make this sound, they slowly rise, following with their eyes the invisible steeply rising jet which leaves them, finally, looking off left. Squatting, they held their arms stretched out in front of them; rising, they made their arms wings; fully risen and on tiptoe now, they hold their arms down and in closer to their bodies, forming delta shapes. Abruptly now, they switch their heads to look high up off right. Spotting something falling from there, they say:

ALL: sssssssssssssssssssssSSSSSSSSSS!!!

As the hiss increases in volume, they bring their hands down from high over their heads, then bring their hands and arms horizontally bent in front of their bodies down and down, falling themselves at the same time until they are as far down as they can get. Then, putting their hands to their ears, they roar:

ALL: BOOOM!!!

And explode upward in a great spring. Then, megaphones to mouths:

ALL: Ccchhhristian sssoldiers!!! ZIM ZAM ZOOM!!!

The COACH then moves to stage center and blows his whistle and then gives a tone—hums it. The reporters promptly move into position, forming a cross with the COACH—the tallest of the group—as its upstage top. Three increasingly shorter reporters form the rest of the upstage-downstage vertical beam. Two other reporters serve as the arms of the cross. These flanking reporters extend arms to touch the shoulders of the pivot man just in front of the COACH. *Members of the vertical beam lay hands on the shoulders of the person in front of them, while the foot-of-the-cross man, closest to the audience, extends his arms to form yet another cross. They assume this position in a trice, then start singing "Onward Christian Soldiers," pumping their knees in stationary march rhythm as they sing. Recorded orchestral and choral support may provide additional fervor. They tramp there for a time, then may wheel into various other ecclesiastical shapes, etc. When the proper time comes, they line up in a row again, still pumping their knees; the music fades, and they hum. The lights have long since calmed down. Now only one spot lights stage center just ahead of the line formed by the* COACH *and reporters. The marching stops, though the humming of the hymn continues, as* CLAYMORE *steps out of line and into the spot.*

CLAYMORE: There were misunderstandings from the word
  go.
They insisted the game they were already playing
was an ancient form of basketball,
a form similar to that played in Mexico
long before Colombo arrived—a sacred form
at the conclusion of which
the losers lost their heads.
Our team arrived prepared to play football.
Our advisers in the field had warned us
it would be a rough game.
They had failed to mention the exact nature
of the game.
As I say, there was confusion
from the start.

CLAYMORE *steps back into line as* NORDEN *steps out.*

NORDEN: When they saw what was happening,
    the referees either left the field in disgust
    or joined in the mayhem.
    After five minutes in that jungle of mud
    the refs that remained were indistinguishable
    from the rest of the players. Still, some,
    out of habit, called foul when the ball was kicked
    while others waved their hands and blew
    their whistles when the ball was dribbled.
    Each side played with a different-shaped ball—
    one, ovoid; the other, a perfect sphere.

    NORDEN *steps back into line as* GORE *and* GEIGER *step out.*

GORE (*his voice more natural now*): Sometimes three balls
        were in play,
    occasionally four.
GEIGER: In the resulting confusion
    fist fights were as common as
    clap in the barracks. Soon,
    fists weren't enough. Switch blades
    and razors settled things faster.
    They ensured a more lasting
    tranquility.
GORE: Then helicopters, hired out by boosters
    of all teams involved, appeared over the field,
    dropping less primitive weapons.
    Unnecessary roughness was no longer penalized
    or, rather, it was punished by shooting
    a fixed number of spectators sitting up
    in the grandstand like sitting ducks.
    First, one; then three, then seven, then

all you could hit with one clip.

GEIGER: The crowd in the grandstand
   panicked, trampled each other to death
   in their rush for the exits which the local police
   promptly blocked.
   After a time, the dead formed a wall
   blocking the exits far more effectively
   than any police force. The surge
   turned back.

GEIGER *and* GORE *step back into line as* NORDEN *steps
out.*

NORDEN: One muscular spectator, hit
   by a beer bottle dropped from a chopper,
   hurled it back up, denting a rotor.
   It was then hell really broke loose.
   Flying upside down, the choppers came in
   low over the grandstand, slicing
   heads off like so many dandelions
   caught in a lawnmower. Their blades
   were scarlet as suns as they rose up
   at the end of their first run to turn
   to return for a second.

NORDEN *steps back into line as* CLAYMORE, MRS. ASH-
LAND, *and* GEIGER *step out.*

CLAYMORE: Above the screams, above the sound
   of the motors and the crackle of small-arms
   fire out on the field, you could hear
   the lunatic peeps of homemade whistles—
   fingers in mouths, blades of grass, tops
   of beer bottles—as old men and women
   and even children tried to call a halt
   to the game. They lacked, however,

authority to do so. Leaving the exits
from which exit was no longer possible,
platoons of police briskly rounded
these agitators up or, for ready identification
at some later time, split open their skulls.

MRS. ASHLAND: One police-sergeant, recognizing an instant
too late that he had cleft his own mother's skull,
was promptly promoted for having
done his duty regardless.
Refusing the citation, the sergeant was shot for—
quote—
setting himself up as an individual, endangering
thereby
the morale of the force as a whole—end quote.

GEIGER: There were no such slackers in the field.
As the first stringers buckled and fell,
they provided crude breastworks for
the men who replaced them. There was
no longer any limit to the number of
substitutions. In their uniforms of mud,
the living and the dead could no longer
be distinguished one from the other.
Coaches tore their hair on the sidelines.

CLAYMORE: Coaches tore their hair on the sidelines and
openly wept as the cameras rolled by
on the sidelines, as newsmen fed the coaches
with portable mikes, as cables tripped subs
warming up on the sidelines, as the mascots
whined in their baskets, and as cheerleaders,
roaring through megaphones, jack-knifed
high in the air, exposing the whites of their
crotches and the sharp uncompromising cones
of their breasts. "Don't let us down!" they cried.
Two were wounded in action.

NORDEN steps out to join CLAYMORE, ASHLAND, *and* GEIGER. *Only* GORE *and the* COACH *hum now.*

NORDEN: Meanwhile, the coach of the visiting team relayed
 his order out to the field: Outflank their defense,
 capture the hoop and put up a goal post fast
 to make everything clear and more perfectly
 legal. His towering halfback, however,
 rising up for a look, then saw for the first time
 since the start of the game that crowd,
 that leftover crowd that still jammed
 the grandstand, and he screamed:
 "Call the game off! Look! Nobody's watching!"
MRS. ASHLAND: And it was true.
 The audience that lay or sat stacked by the
 hundred, the thousand, the ten thousand, millions,
 was either headless or cut off through the chest
 or down to the waist or legs in a row
 sitting alone on the bleachers and, so,
 could no longer see. Only a handful
 of children, too short to be cut down
 with the rest, remained to observe a game
 they could not understand.

GORE *joins the line of reporters. The* COACH, *behind them, is blocked from view except for his gigantic shoulders and lesser head. Only the* COACH *still hums.*

GORE: The game was played, as scheduled
 and as always,
 away from home.
GEIGER: There was a brief pause in the fighting
 on both sides of the field.

The COACH *hums the last line of the hymn solo. He then walks around one end of the line of reporters, slowly. Then he stops, smiles, and looks out as if test-ing the atmosphere, then walks on further downstage. He limbers himself up as he walks—loosens up his shoulders, gets the kinks out of his legs.*

COACH (*to the audience*): Know one thing though? (*He does a knee bend.*) We never lost a single game yet? (*He rises, then does another knee bend. His voice is calm, kind, friendly, soft.*) But folks elsewhere. . . . How crazy can they get? (*He rises.*) They take us on and they never even heard of . . . (*Cocking his right arm as if about to throw a long pass—a stance that makes him look a good deal like the Statue of Liberty —the* COACH, *fondly smiling, lets his gesture speak for itself.*)

The line of reporters, meanwhile, has lifted, in slow motion, the red megaphones. Giving voice to the COACH'S *gesture, they say:*

REPORTERS (*in hoarse, slow, dejected unison*): Football.

END

Fireworks for a Hot Fourth
a three-in-one-act passion play

This play was first performed at a staged reading at the Eugene O'Neill Memorial Theater Foundation on July 19, 1968, directed by J Ranelli. The cast was as follows:

GROWTH	Joseph Shaw
GLORIA	Diana Douglas
ANNA	Patricia Elliot
BELLE	Pat Cohen
OLD LOCAL	Joseph Attles
SIDNEY	Bernard Kates
HAROLD	Tom Adkins

CHARACTERS
(*in order of appearance*)

GROWTH, *a stocky man in his late fifties*
GLORIA, *Growth's wife; a lean woman in her early fifties*
ANNA, *a beautiful young woman, blonde*
BELLE, *a beautiful young woman, dark-haired; Sidney's wife*
OLD LOCAL, *a lean, weathered man of about seventy*
SIDNEY, *a man in his mid-thirties*
HAROLD, *a moon-faced man of about thirty-seven*

> NOTE: *Anna and Belle are two visions of the*
> *same woman and should look, move,*
> *and be dressed accordingly.*

THE STAGE

The large living room of a house by the sea in a town on an island like Long Island. Picture windows take up almost the entire upstage wall area. The view looks out to sea and sky. At the beginning, the gray sky still glows with the red of sunset. Against this view—which could be an enormously blown-up black and white (and, for a time, red) photograph as three-dimensional as the Kodak display in Grand Central Station—people, or at least silhouettes and profiles of people, holding glasses, standing in clusters, can be seen. There may be as many as thirty, even forty "people" in this room—most of them represented by display window manikins or tailor's dummies or cutouts or plaster casts of people, stray statues, etc.

Especially at the very start—when nobody is moving anyway—these dummies, etc., look as real as the people, or as unreal. Throughout, they remain in the fringes of light, appearing only as sharp or dim shadows. The effect of the scene as a whole should be grainy, like a black-and-white movie—since the only colors used are black, white, and various shades of gray.

Almost everyone in the room smokes. As the play goes on, the room gets steadily smokier.

A stylized conversational drone—like the one which opens the play—may be used, at times, at various pitches.

Before the curtain rises, a band can be heard playing the opening bars of "My Country, 'Tis of Thee," loud at first, then diminishing in volume. As the curtain rises, the music fades and merges into a loud beehive drone of stylized conversation. The stage is lit by a dim evening light—the light behind the people brighter than the light in the room. The drone drops as a light picks up GROWTH *and* GLORIA— *each holding a drink,* GLORIA *smoking—downstage center.*

GROWTH: We asked them for drinks and now nobody's
    leaving.
  It's time for supper and nobody's moving.
  All they're doing is standing and drinking.
  Aren't they ever planning to leave?
GLORIA: Go away.
GROWTH: I beg your pardon?
GLORIA: If you have to grumble, don't do it by me.
  Why don't you just go away?
GROWTH: By George
  and I will someday. You treat me like this
  —you'll see.
GLORIA: You won't, you know.
GROWTH: Of course I won't. This is my own house,
  isn't it? Well, answer me. Isn't it?

GLORIA: Does renting a house make it yours?
   Does having a wife mean you're married?
GROWTH: What?
GLORIA: Does being alive mean you're living?
GROWTH: What? I don't know. I don't know.
   I'm deeply troubled by all this.

As GROWTH *moves out of the light and away,* ANNA *and* BELLE *move into the light from stage left. Dressed as twins, they move as twins but generally back to back as if completely unaware of each other. While* ANNA *faces* GLORIA, BELLE *looks off left.*

GLORIA (*to* ANNA): How lovely to see you again!
   How lovely to see you again!
   How lovely how lovely how lovely how lovely
   how lovely to see you again.
   I remember your face as if it was yesterday.
   I'm afraid I've forgotten your name.

ANNA's *reply is drowned out by the sound of breaking glass and a burst of laughter from the rear of the room.* BELLE *glances at her face in a pocket mirror.* ANNA *turns as* BELLE *turns toward* GLORIA, *and, moving behind* BELLE, *vanishes.* GLORIA *speaks to* BELLE.

   Who did she say she was, Belle?
BELLE: I'm afraid
   I don't know . . . I don't know who you mean.
   I thought I was here all alone.
GLORIA: How tactless of me. How tactful of you
   not to see her at all. It was that
   Hanna or something from Islip or somewhere
   your husband's been after all afternoon.
   Poor dear. You stand right where you are.

There must be at least one unattached male
who'd love . . .

BELLE: Gloria, don't. I'd really prefer . . .

GLORIA: I won't be a minute. Stand right where you are.
(*She moves out of the light and away.*)

BELLE: I feel very uncomfortable standing here all alone.
I shall feel very uncomfortable if somebody comes.
I simply feel very . . .

The OLD LOCAL *enters the light.*

Are you going to make me uncomfortable?

OLD LOCAL: Not in the old days. Not this way in the old
days at all.

A seat is served up under him. The OLD LOCAL *sits.*
BELLE *sits on the floor slightly to one side and in front
of him as he talks.*

The Glorious Fourth. That's what we called it then
and it was.

Parades. Real parades. Whole town turned out in
those days

and people far off used to come. I should know. I
should know.

Been in 'em all since I was a boy. I was a drummer boy.

Man with a flute, man with a bandaged head and a
flag and me

with my drum up in front of a band—with a crowd—
a parade

and the judges all up in their stand—a man could be
proud of today and I am.

Then, O, back about five, six years ago, I was Ben
Franklin,

white wig and specs on. Looked just like him they say.

Now they're off to the moon or whatever they're up to,

but fireworks on the Fourth, they're not what they
    used to be,
they're not what they used to be, that's one thing for
    sure.
Great shows they used to put on. Whole street filled
    up and the sky.
Been in 'em all since I was a boy. I was a drummer boy.

You take this town now. It's changed too. A man lives
    his life out
in a hick town like this, don't really reconize any more
with the elms all down in the first place,
and the fields to the east used to hunt with my dad
    and the woods,
the woods we tramped every fall, all down, cleared off
    and leveled,
and up go those houses one by one in a row,
every one like the next or a baby pink door for a
    change—
it troubles a man, it makes a man think,
it makes a man wonder just what he stayed put for
in the place he grew up in when it changes like that,
and everything's changing, that's one thing for sure.

Take me now, take me for instance.
I'm born and bred and nowhere at home in my own
    home town any more.
Uncle of mine used to own this place, cousin got hold
    of it now,
lets it out to folks out from the city,
come for the shore I suppose, people I don't hardly
    know,
and I always come back to this place once a year that
    I knew,

ast me over for drinks and I put in a show,
have a drink for the Fourth, then ready to go.
Don't know why they ast me, don't know why I come
since what's there to say people don't know like I do
  the past
of the place or the sea? They're here for a summer
  where I was a boy.
But they always ast me, and over I come, and why not?
(*He looks at his glass, which is empty, then rises with*
BELLE's *help.*)
I like to keep up traditions.

He takes BELLE's *arm. The light on them dims and
goes out as they move off into the crowd and as,
promptly, another light picks up* SIDNEY *and* ANNA—
*stage left—on a small raised platform, perhaps a bal-
cony. On this platform, a reclining chair.*

SIDNEY: Beautiful woman. Beautiful Swede. Anna.
I've found you the only chair in the room.
Aren't you at least going to thank me, Anna?
ANNA: Thank you, Sidney.
SIDNEY: You're welcome, Anna.
Do you mind my calling you Anna
since you refuse to tell me your name
or even if you do come from Sweden?
ANNA: Whatever you want, my dear.
SIDNEY: How obliging you are
and how strange to find you at last and here
of all places, hovering over
the grave of this room like the last angel.
Look at them. They have eyes but see not.
I saw you the minute I came into this room.
How on earth, or how in hell I should say,
did you get into this gasser anyway?

ANNA: I'm not sure, Sidney, what a gasser is.
SIDNEY: Of course not, Swede. I'm sorry. I do.
It's ... it's a smile without a face, to begin with,
then multiplied by forty—and this.
Or simply people with nothing to say
saying it constantly. Or an office,
a day at an office spent earning the money
for a short escape from that office,
as I and half of the dead in this room do too.
Each and every one of these is,
in its own individual way,
an additional gas in the atmosphere.
So how did you come to be here, Anna—
if you don't mind my calling you Anna.
ANNA: I was down on the beach when somebody called
from the house and I came up to the door
and he went for a drink
(*A dim light picks up* HAROLD *handing* GLORIA *a drink
by the bar upstage right. As they move out of the
light, the* OLD LOCAL *and* BELLE *enter it.*)
and never returned.
He was odd. He was sad. I was glad
he never returned. Who's that old man?
SIDNEY: An old man and a bore, I'm afraid.
ANNA: And the woman with him who looks lonely?
SIDNEY: Yes. I guess you could say she looks lonely—
in fact, lonely enough to be my wife
if, in fact, I had a wife.
ANNA: Are you married,
Sidney?
SIDNEY: I have a wife, yes.
ANNA (*standing back a bit in the shadows*): I see.
SIDNEY: You do? I don't. She's lost in the crowd, I'm afraid.

The light now excludes ANNA, *brightens on* SIDNEY.
The light by the bar now excludes the OLD LOCAL,
brightening—though still dim—on BELLE.

Or lost in the crowd of days, I'm afraid.

I'm afraid   I'm afraid
I'm afraid   I'm afraid
I'm afraid it's time to wake up.
It's time to wake up.   (*Gradual crescendo.*)
it's time to wash up
it's time to brush up
it's time to come down   (*Decrescendo.*)
for bréakfust.

Good morning good morning
good morning   good morning
good morning   good morning
good morning.
BELLE: Good morning, Sidney.
SIDNEY: Well
    and now I'm afraid
    and now I'm afraid
    it's time for me to be óff now.
BELLE: Already?
SIDNEY: O it's hígh tíme for me to be off
    I'm afraid   I'm afraid
    I'm afraid   I'm afraid
    unless I'm going to be late.
BELLE: Good-bye, Sidney.
SIDNEY: Good-bye, Belle,
    my darling
    (*The light on* BELLE *is now almost out, while the light
    on* SIDNEY *begins to include* ANNA *again.*)
    my hope

(*The light on* BELLE *is out.*)
my desire.

ANNA *stands next to* SIDNEY. *They hold hands. As the
light on them slowly fades, another light picks up*
GLORIA, *downstage center; she is leading* HAROLD *downstage. He carries a drink in each hand.*

GLORIA: I can't imagine where she could be.
　　　　She promised to wait right here.
HAROLD: I don't mind.
GLORIA: What do you mean you don't mind?
HAROLD: Well, maybe
　　　　I don't want to meet her again áfter all
　　　　after lugging these drinks for an hour
　　　　trying to find her myself in this crowd.
GLORIA: We must be talking about two different people.
HAROLD: A girl I called up from the shore. Up near,
　　　　she looked like an actress but smelled like a . . .
GLORIA: We must be talking about two different people.
HAROLD: Then might I suggest we talk about you?
　　　　It was you anyway I wanted to meet.
　　　　I took just one look at you and I thought . . .
　　　　I want you to know by the way from the start
　　　　I'm a Certified Public Accountant.
　　　　I work in the city of course and I've done
　　　　considerable work for our genial host.
　　　　I trust you know Mr. Growth since you're here.
GLORIA: You have, I must say, a certain style.
HAROLD: I'm glad you like to think so. Thank you.
GLORIA: I don't know what you're so grateful for.
　　　　I didn't say what kind of style.
HAROLD: That's true.
GLORIA: You also have a certain look.

HAROLD: I do?
What kind, if you don't mind my asking?
GLORIA: Ask away.

She dunks one cigarette out in her glass, puts the glass down or hands it to HAROLD, *and takes another cigarette from a small handbag or cigarette cartridge belt.*

HAROLD: All right. What kind of look do I have?
GLORIA: You really want to know? Are you sure?
HAROLD: I believe I do. Don't bother to flatter.
GLORIA: Hang-dog, whipped, a good scout but harried.
A little man on a short leash.
You look as if you were going to get married
any minute now, and love it.
HAROLD: I'm not though.
GLORIA: Not though what?
HAROLD: Planning to marry.
GLORIA: Well bully for you! Then act like a gentleman
and light my cigarette, will you?
HAROLD: Of course.
Delighted. You care for a . . .
(*He hands her one of his drinks and lights her cigarette for her.*)
And you?
Are you by any chance if you'll excuse
my asking married yourself by the way?
GLORIA: What would you say?
HAROLD: I'm afraid I'd have to say yes.
GLORIA: You're afraid you'd have to say yes, are you?
Well, you'd be dead right too—dead right and an ass
for saying so and an ass for being so
and if only you knew, if you only . . .

A dim light picks up GROWTH. *Glass in hand, he is facing a cluster of heads upstage right. He stands on a chair or a stool, holding forth.*

GROWTH: Thomas E. Dewey wanted to be President.
Harold Stassen wanted to be President.
Wendell L. Willkie wanted to be President.
Richard Milhous Nixon wanted to be President so bad
he could—and the entire patriotic American public
    right along with him
could—taste it.
None of them became President.
Instead, our present President is President.
What I want to know is, what's wrong with the Ameri-
    can people anyway?
What I want to say is, if you can't grow up, keep mov-
    ing—grow *out!*
That's the message I'd like to leave behind.
(*The light on him dims somewhat.*)
Still, I don't know. I don't know.
I don't know what to do
I don't know who I am
except what I have, except what I own,
and furthermore who are all these people?

The light on him goes out. The light on GLORIA *and* HAROLD *dims slowly as they speak.*

GLORIA: I don't even know your name.
HAROLD: Harold.
GLORIA: I don't know anyone named Harold.
I don't want to know anyone named Harold.
If your name really is Harold, then please
just run along now like a good boy.
HAROLD: You're extremely cruel, do you know that?

GLORIA: Yes. I know, and you know it too, and I know
    something else. You love it. Admit it. You do.
HAROLD: Why else would I follow you around like this?
GLORIA: See? I knew. I know your kind. Don't get me wrong.
    There are many but, still, many too few. Yes.
    We may get along if . . .
    (*Inhaling deeply.*)
    Here.
    (*Taking the cigarette out of her mouth.*)
    Look.
    (*Holding out the burning cigarette end.*)
    Kiss.
    This.

HAROLD, *looking at her, bows and kisses the hot end of
the cigarette as the light on them fades out. A slight
hissing sound. The stage remains unlit, the people and
dummies, shadows only, silhouetted against the gray
light of the sea and sky which is seen through the large
windows upstage, as the repeat chorus of Bach's chorale
"O Sacred Head Now Wounded" is played at a brisk
tempo by an orchestra without chorus. As the chorale
concludes, a light picks up* BELLE, GROWTH, *and the*
OLD LOCAL. *They are sitting on three chairs, facing
front, downstage right. As* BELLE *begins to speak. a
dimmer light picks up* SIDNEY *and* ANNA, *still in their
raised stage-left spot.* SIDNEY *is sitting beside* ANNA *on
the reclining chair. She is half-reclining; he, sitting
upright, is frozen in the act of stroking her face or hair.*

BELLE: I loved my husband. He became my brother.
    I loved my brother. He became my son
    and, like a son, full of rebellion.
    I love my husband-brother-son
    but, like a mother,

want to possess him
which, naturally, he can't stand.

The light on SIDNEY *and* ANNA *dims and goes out. As* GROWTH *begins to speak, another light picks up* GLORIA *and* HAROLD, *stage center.* GLORIA *is holding a newly lit cigarette in front of her lips.* HAROLD, *next to her, stands facing out—the four fingers of his right hand are pressed to his lips; his eyes are still large.*

GROWTH: I loved my wife. She became a husband.
I loved my husband. I became a wife.
But, unable to bear children as I constitutionally am,
I feel cross at the office, fed up at home
and, in general, terrified of life.
I don't think she's very fond of it either.

The light on GLORIA *and* HAROLD *goes out.*

Who . . . who . . . who are all these people?
OLD LOCAL: Everything was a lot simpler when I was a boy.
Now that I'm older, I don't understand,
I'm not understood, I guess I'm a bore.
They're off to the moon. There's a war somewhere
that, if I understand right, you can't call a war.
Twice we beat the Germans. Now they're back where
    they were.
Sometimes I think I just better pack up my gear,
stuff some shirts in a sack
and find me a one-room shack
out where there's nobody around but the stripers
and the ducks drop in and there's gulls.
Not that I'd understand them either, I guess.
Then too, I'd have to sell the old place . . .
GROWTH: I'm listening now.
OLD LOCAL: I said I'd have to sell the old place.

GROWTH: You have an old . . . Out here? How many acres?

OLD LOCAL: Well, it's a cousin of mine owns this
    and I have my own place, sure.

GROWTH: A cousin . . . And you . . . Yes. Of course.
    So that's the reason we invite you over!
    (*To* BELLE.)
    Excuse us a minute, will you, miss?
    There's a time for pleasure and a time for business.

As GROWTH *turns to talk to the* OLD LOCAL, BELLE *rises
to go. The light leaves all three of them and picks up*
GLORIA *and* HAROLD *standing midstage, or up, facing
front.*

GLORIA: I who loved power found power was weak,
    a child that cried for protection.
    I who mothered that child grew strong
    for which I was never forgiven.
    I in turn shall never forgive
    or love ever again
    except a sacrifice, willing and fit,
    be offered up for my motherly, loving destruction.
    Then shall it taste hot tears.
    Then shall it be bitten and torn.
    Then shall it be consumed utterly.
    Perhaps then I shall be consumed too,
    shall forgive and shall love and shall die
    pure again as the girl I was
    before I who loved power found it was weak,
    a child that cries for protection.
    (*A chair is served up under her. She sits.*)
    I have, unfortunately, no other children.

HAROLD: For a moment I turned and saw on the beach
    like a dream by the sea and I called
    and she came forward strangely up from the beach

and the closer she came the greater the dread
as I saw her approaching,
the pleasure approaching,
the promise of pleasure at last.
And the nearer it came the greater the dread.
Like a sickness all over my face it spread
and I smiled, feeling the hatred grow.

For one final acceptable time
I have set the moment of pleasure aside
time and again until it has grown a dream
in my head that grows by being denied—
during the day in my work,
in the night in the dark—
until the promise of pleasure has passed,
spat white, out of my hands. Inside,
the night demands one stark crucified bride
who will "No! No!"—feeling my hate sink in.

A chair is served up under HAROLD. *He sits.* BELLE *appears behind* GLORIA.

BELLE: Gloria?
GLORIA (*not quite hearing, not turning; frozen*): Yes.
BELLE: Gloria.
GLORIA (*identifying the voice but not turning*): Belle.
BELLE: I wondered ...

HAROLD *rises slowly from his chair.*

GLORIA: Yes. I'm listening now. I can hear you. But
    I think you'll find Sidney up thére, my dear.
    I'm quite sure you'll find him úp there.
BELLE: I don't want to find him. I know where he is.
    I wanted to give him a chance to play.
    I wanted to meet, I wanted to try.

I wanted to learn to pretend to enjoy . . .

GLORIA: Certainly not this little man—this tedious boy.
Can you guess what his name is? Harold.
You'd better find Sidney, leave this chore to me.

BELLE *moves out of the light and away.*

HAROLD: You . . .
(*He sits.*)

GLORIA: That was the one I brought you to meet.
That was the treat I had in store.
Did she look like an actress or smell like a whore?
Is she the one that waved from the shore?
Did you mind that I sent her away?
Did you mind that I called you a boy?
Did you mind that I laughed at your name?
Did you mind? Did it hurt? Did I hurt you?
If I hurt you, I'm terribly sorry.

HAROLD: Not me. You don't need to worry.

GLORIA: I don't. You'll have your reward . . .
(*She looks at him and puts her hand on his knee.*)

HAROLD (*in the same tone and rhythm, and putting a hand
on Gloria's knee*): You'll have your reward . . .

GLORIA and HAROLD: You'll have your reward in good time.

The light leaves them and picks up GROWTH *and the*
OLD LOCAL *downstage right—*GROWTH *is standing, the*
OLD LOCAL *sitting.*

GROWTH: If your five acres is frontage acres,
and if you want to sell, as you say—
then look, it stands to reason.

And if this place is insured to the hilt,
and all your cousin wants is me to do him a favor—
look here. I'm a reasonable man.

I do him a favor. You do me a favor.
All three, we do us a favor.
Follow? It all stands to reason.

BELLE *is seen for an instant wedging her way between
the Old Local's chair and the forms in the crowd
behind her.* GROWTH *speaks to* BELLE.

Hello there.
(*Forgetting* BELLE; *back to the* OLD LOCAL.)
Twenty houses where there was two.
You and your cousin each get what you want,
I get what I'm after too and, moreover,
we do twenty new families a favor!

OLD LOCAL: Everything was a lot simpler when I was a boy.
Now that I'm older I don't understand,
I'm not understood, I guess I'm a bore.
They're off to the moon. There's a war somewhere
that, if I understand right, you can't call a war.
Twice we beat the Germans. Now they're back where
    they were.
Sometimes I think I just better pack up my gear . . .

GROWTH: Precisely. Now look.
(*Before squatting down beside the* OLD LOCAL, GROWTH
glances quickly around him. To himself.)
Who are all these people?
(*Then, once again, to the* OLD LOCAL.)
I'll go through the whole thing once more.

The light leaves GROWTH *and the* OLD LOCAL, *picking
up* SIDNEY *and* ANNA *in their raised spot stage left.*
SIDNEY—*standing, facing front—is in the center of the
light while* ANNA, *at first, remains in the shadows. As*
SIDNEY *begins to speak, a dim light catches* BELLE, *up-*

stage center and a bit to the left, glass in hand, apparently talking to a silhouette.

SIDNEY: I loved my wife as nobody does these days
or, certainly, few.
After long experience, none of which I regret
and which aways seemed new
to me as I grazed through a field of sighs
undoing brassieres,
I lost my way. I was naked. I was wet
with somebody's tears.

I stood near the middle. But where had I come in?
And how get out
of that field around which I now saw sharp wires,
in which sighs turned to shout
and cry, and friendly love to bitter passion.
And as I stood—
each way looking alike lost to my eyes and desires—
she appeared at one edge of that field,
waving, and also naked, also wet, also beautiful.
And I ran.
Where we met—she on one side, I on the other—
where we began
the wires ended and there were trees and it was fall.
I still believe,
I still relive, I still recall those days in which, together,
we often lost to refind our love.

After the field, the wood. After the wood, a road.
At the end of the road,
a city. I have sometimes returned to the field.
It has been plowed.
I have never been back to the woods, I'm afraid.

The light on BELLE *dims, going out when the dialogue begins below.*

Are they still there?
Sun, shade, even apples. An Eden. Probably leveled.
And, since then, a cheerful despair.

The light grows, in the last line above, to include
ANNA, *who is sitting on the reclining chair, her legs up on it, the chair tilted back only slightly.*

And the strangest thing is— Are you listening?
ANNA: Yes.
SIDNEY: The strangest thing is that, as a result
    of no longer expecting pleasure,
    perhaps of no longer deserving it either,
    leading the servile lucrative lives we do,
    I can hardly believe in it when it's there.
    In fact, my dear, I'm not sure I'm sure
    either you or I is actually here.
    Are you?
ANNA: Not at all.
SIDNEY: Odd, to be so much a part of the atmosphere
    and yet, when I breathe myself in,
    feel less alive than before.
    But this is, I'm afraid, very selfish of me.
    Of course, you, coming from your far country, here,
    must feel that even more strongly. I mean
    you do feel like a foreigner, don't you?
ANNA: Very much, dear.
SIDNEY: Of course. How strange. And yet here
    of all places we have to meet
    where one can only enjoy people talking.
    One can't whisper and still be heard in this roar
    One can't make love as one could on a shore.

One can't shed clothes, unleash the brassiere.
One can only enjoy people talking here.
(*In an affectionate, bantering, social tone, slowly be-*
ginning to play the part of an analyst. Rising, perhaps
pacing.)
Tell me,
when did it first come over you,
this feeling of alienation?

ANNA: Are you this much a part of your atmosphere?

SIDNEY: Anna, I am. This is my cheerful despair.
Then, too, how will I ever know me
if I haven't, my dear, known you? So.
Answer me, darling.
(*He tilts the back of the chair so far back that* ANNA
is stretched out as if on an analyst's couch. He stares
down at her, one hand holding the chair down.)
When? When you left home?

ANNA: When I left home.

SIDNEY: When you stepped off a boat, when you came here?

ANNA: When I stepped off a boat, when I came here.

SIDNEY: When you entered a door, when you met me?

ANNA: When I entered a door, when I met you,
all, then, I began to feel strange. Will that do?

SIDNEY: That boat—so obviously a symbol
of the womb, that boat. One is, after all,
borne through the water in a . . . You weren't,
by any chance, born in a boat were you, Anna?

ANNA: No.

SIDNEY: Then where on earth wére you born?

ANNA: On the grass, in a wood—a beautiful wood.

SIDNEY: On the grass, in a wood—a beautiful wood,
in a far-away country called Sweden.
Men dream of the women there, Anna.

And what . . . what . . . what language did you speak
    there?

ANNA: It must have been Swedish, Sidney.

SIDNEY: Ah child, then can't you see
    how simple the whole thing is?
    For as many years as you've lived, I'm afraid,
    you've lived in a dream-world neurosis.
    You must be completely addicted,
    completely at home in that country by now
    with its fantasy language to match.
    I suppose there's a king in your country?

ANNA: There is.

SIDNEY: Of course. And a handsome prince
    as well, no doubt. And you've been waked by a kiss.

ANNA: Yes. And waked others with kisses too.

SIDNEY: And is there a war going on there at present?

ANNA: No war.

SIDNEY: And the name of this country is?

ANNA: Sweden?

SIDNEY: Say it in Swedish, please.

ANNA: I can't.

SIDNEY: Yes. Then one final question, dear,
    from your lover dissolving in his atmosphere,
    how do you get there? Quick!
    The shortest route. The quickest way over.

ANNA: I just close my eyes. Try closing your own.
    I'll help you.
    (*She rises, puts her hands, from behind, over Sidney's
    eyes, kisses him, and steps back, taking her hands off
    his eyes, which are now shut. She stands half in
    shadow.*)

SIDNEY: I have closed my eyes. I begin to see.
    I have closed my eyes. I begin. I see.
    I'm afraid all I see, my dear, is a door.

(*He feels the door with his hands, like a blindman.*)
An elevator door, I believe.
Which is opening now, all by itself.
There's nobody in it. I'm in it.
ANNA: Sidney. Sidney, my dear.
SIDNEY: There's music now. Listen. There's music.
Nobody's playing it but it's playing.
More people are crowding in now. The doors
are closing though nobody's touched them.
They're shut now.
ANNA: Sidney. Good-bye.
(*The light no longer includes her.*)
SIDNEY: We're moving now. Moving up.
Nobody moves the machine I can see but
we're moving up anyway. People smile.
They don't look too happy but they're smiling
as we take the first twenty floors without stopping,
and the door that nobody touches opens,
and as I excuse me I'm smiling too
as the doors close on music nobody plays.
I'm walking now, down a hall.
There's an oval desk with a woman behind it.
She smiles at me and I smile too.
There's a turn in the hall and I take it.
There's an office door to which I have a key
and I open the door all by myself
and see somebody's in it already who's turning.
He's looking my way and now I can see
his smile as he turns . . . as he turns in his chair
smiling at me and, by God! That smile! It's me!
A VOICE: Sidney. It isn't.
SIDNEY: Who put me in there!
A VOICE: Sidney.

SIDNEY (*suddenly calm, as if nothing had happened*): May
I open my eyes now, Anna?

The light expands to show BELLE *who, from behind,
puts her hands on Sidney's forehead.*

BELLE: Please do.
(*She takes her hands off Sidney's head and stands by
his side.*)
SIDNEY (*opening his eyes*): Belle. Yes, of course. Dear Belle.

The light on SIDNEY *and* BELLE *goes out. The stage
remains unlit, the people and dummies, shadows only,
silhouetted against the gray light of the sea and sky
are seen through the large windows upstage. Bach's
chorale "Befiehl Du, deine Wege" is played at a brisk
tempo by an orchestra without chorus. As the chorale
concludes, three lights simultaneously pick out* 1) *the*
OLD LOCAL *and* GROWTH, *who is using a telephone,
stage right;* 2) GLORIA *and* HAROLD *in the raised area
downstage left where* SIDNEY *and* BELLE *stood before;
and* 3) SIDNEY *and* BELLE, *stage center, standing—*
SIDNEY *facing front,* BELLE *facing* SIDNEY. *For the
short time the light remains on all three groups, all
remain motionless. When the lights on the* OLD LOCAL
and GROWTH *and on* GLORIA *and* HAROLD *dim and perhaps go out,* SIDNEY *begins to speak.*

I am not sure I will ever be able to forgive you
for not being able to see you daily and constantly
in the full light—the fire—of my desire for you.
It is a crime which crumbles eternity into minutes.
It is a crime whose punishment is the dim-lit half-lived
    life
of this room. It straps me to a clock of predictable
    days,

a clock which, to all men, says the same thing.
Hearing it daily, I have learned it by heart.
Living with me, you too have learned it. Say it.
BELLE: *Midnight and noon my scissors click.*
Men sigh.
Things unimagined live by the clock,
live by the clock and die.
SIDNEY: Because my passion is frequently unsteady, divided,
because my life is divided between essential routine
and the lessening seconds of impractical ecstasy,
because we are, together, bound to the same deadly clock,
often we twist to punish each other for sharing that fate,
and, unable to see each other constantly
in the full light, the fire, the blaze,
we create a deadly smoke, we long for the ashes at least—
our passion, a passion for ashes.

It's good to see you again, old girl.
BELLE: It's lovely to find you. If you only knew ...
SIDNEY: Perhaps I do.
(*Taking out a cigarette case.*)
Perhaps I remind you
(*Offering* BELLE *a cigarette. She takes one.* SIDNEY *takes one too.*)
of a husband you had once. Right?
BELLE: Sidney.
SIDNEY: I only say that because, vaguely,
(*Smiling, lighting her cigarette.*)
beautiful as you are, and you are—
you remind me of a wife. No. It's true.

(*Lighting his own.*)

BELLE: I know. That's why I left you. Do we
always have to act this way at a . . . ?

SIDNEY: I'm afraid . . . I'm afraid
we do. It's in the atmosphere.

BELLE: What's in the atmosphere?

SIDNEY: Why, me—my darling—and you.

> *The light leaves* SIDNEY *and* BELLE, *picking up* GROWTH
> —*talking into a telephone in a low voice while light-*
> *ing a fat cigar—and the* OLD LOCAL, *now holding a fat*
> *cigar.*

GROWTH (*aloud*): Who? Me! I'll attend to it personly.
I've got the means right here at my fingertips.
I'll attend to it personly. Good-bye.
(*Hangs up.*)
You'd think the place was already lit,
what with the smoke in this room.
(*To the* OLD LOCAL.)
It's settled.

OLD LOCAL (*leaning in for a light*): What say?

GROWTH: Your cousin. Your cousin. Gave his O.K.
Insurance paid up. It's all settled.

OLD LOCAL: He used to be in 'em too. Great shows. Whole
street filled up and the sky.

GROWTH: I say, I get this place *and* yours,
it's all settled.

OLD LOCAL: Since I was a boy.
Been in 'em all. But you take this town now. It's
changed. A man lives
his life out in a small town like this. . . .

GROWTH:You're moving. Don't you get it? You can move.

OLD LOCAL: . . . don't hardly recognize
the place any more, with the elms all down

GROWTH *starts writing out a check.*

and the fields to the east used to hunt with my dad
      and the woods
we tramped every fall—all cleared off, leveled,
and up go those houses one by one in a row . . .
GROWTH: Exactly. Twenty houses where there was two.
      And for you there's that one-room shack by the sea.
      From this minute on, old timer,
      (*he tears out a check and hands it to the* OLD LOCAL)
                                          it's yours.
OLD LOCAL: I see. Well. Thanks very much. Lovely party.
      Tell you one thing though before leaving.
      Better clear out the people 'fore
      you start any trouble.
GROWTH: People? Who *are* all these people?
OLD LOCAL: Another thing, too, better hold in mind.
      Today's a poor day set fire to a place.
      First there's the bands marching straight through town.
      Then all the firemen, they're in the parade.
      I should know. I should know. Been in 'em all.
      I was a drummer boy. Well (*he rises to go;* GROWTH
          rises too, a hand out for good-byes), thanks very
          much and good-bye.

The light leaves GROWTH *and the* OLD LOCAL *shaking
hands. Another light picks up* GLORIA *and* HAROLD *in
their raised stage-left spot.*

GLORIA (*accepting a light from* HAROLD): Why do I smoke
          so much? Why do you think
      I smoke so much?
HAROLD: You're on edge, I suppose.
      I make you a bit on edge.
GLORIA: How clever

you are and how wrong. How stupid you are
and enchanting. How ugly you are
and how lovely. How manly you are, my son.
No. Just look. It's burning between my fingers.
I'm sitting here, sitting here talking,
but while I sit here, sitting here talking,
doing the nothing I do every day,
unable to hope, unable to pray,
unable to laugh, unable to cry,
waiting to live, waiting to die,
doing the nothing I do every day,
it's doing—and what is it doing?
It's burning. It's burning. I'm smoking.
I'm doing something, can't you see *that?*
I'm *do*ing something. I'm smoking.

HAROLD: I see.
But when, say, you put a cigarette out,
what happens then?

GLORIA: What happens then?
For the minute between, I'm dead.

HAROLD: I don't smoke, myself.

GLORIA: No. I can see that.
It's written, darling, all over your face,
all over your body, all over your head.
What's the next world like, anyway, Harry?

HAROLD: What do you mean? I didn't say *I* was dead!

GLORIA: They never do, the darlings; never know.
That's why they are what they are, Harry.

HAROLD: Good night!

GLORIA: Poor sweet terrified Harry.
You're not quite ready to believe me,
are you, love? Not quite. Hold on.
(*She unzips the back of her dress, and, rising, takes*
HAROLD *by the arm.*)

Come with me, Harry. We'll prove it.

HAROLD (*grimly pulling* GLORIA *around to face him*): So
 you're the one. So be it.

The light on GLORIA *and* HAROLD *goes out, leaving the
stage unlit, the people and dummies, shadows only, silhouetted against the gray light of the sea and sky as
seen through the large windows upstage. The drone
of conversation is heard, rising, and a crackling. As a
band is heard playing, first at a distance then closer
and closer, Sousa's "Stars and Stripes Forever," the
crackling sound grows louder, the drone of conversation rises to a roar, and the stage is suffused with the
smoke-threaded red glow of fire.*

CURTAIN

Short Sacred Rite
of Search and
Destruction
a play in seven scenes

CHARACTERS
(in order of appearance)

WALTER, *the father*
DOCTOR, *Walter's friend*
MARION, *Walter's woman*
EDWARD, *Walter's younger son*

NOTES ON THE CHARACTERS

WALTER is forty-eight years old, heavy but well built. He
is about six feet three. In spite of his bulk, he moves
lightly—a man who keeps in trim by playing tennis,
swimming, and sailing. He has a good head of hair.
A senior partner in an important law firm, Walter
specializes in corporation tax law. He comes from
Ohio originally, a forefather homesteaded there in the
early 19th century. (The old homestead—built by a
restless ancestor who took off from Vermont—is still
standing, though grown vast with additions. A twenty-
odd room house, it had to be mortgaged to the hilt
after the banks crashed. Walter's father was a Republi-
can banker who, though ruined, insisted on paying up
on all accounts—a process which lasted from 1929 to
1947.) But Walter doesn't feel very Midwestern. Only
a certain strain of raw energy keeps him from being
mistaken for an Easterner by an Easterner. Details of
his marriage emerge throughout the play. Early joy
turned to mature disaffection. His attraction to his late
wife, Louisa, and hers to him, can perhaps best be
summed up in these lines:

> The passionate sea, longing for limits,
> caresses the cliff.

The cliff, pulverized,
enters its dream.

Walter longed for some restraint to his superabundant
energy; Louisa was refreshed and quickened by it,
until struck by its full cumulative impact. It took years
to reveal itself in its fullness. But what can a man do?
Subdue himself to a genial evenness which bores
everybody, including himself, but wears well in the
long run or seems to? Keep a stable of fillies like
Frenchmen of yore? Not Walter. With his moral up-
bringing, his sincerity, his need to plunge in in depth
rather than spreading himself horizontally, he's as
much a one-woman man as he can manage to be. And
as for subduing himself, no. Proud of his vigor, Walter
loves exercising it, wielding it, and is surprised—when
he stops to notice such things—that others are so
quickly wounded by what he feels is merely a bracing
flow of vital spirits. True, he also blusters to shout
down a profound kind of silence within him which
quietly denies the importance of most of his active,
keyed-up, bustling, successful life. It is as if, in the
midst of a metropolis stacked up like gigantic knives
to scrape out the womb of heaven—or New York, in
short—one green grape-arbor, like the one behind the
Ohio homestead, had miraculously survived, making
the whole show-off show look like nothing more than
a colossal waste of men, time, money, and material. Or
as if the child had survived in the man.

DOCTOR is close to sixty. He has been a close friend of
    Walter, his wife, and their two sons for years. He
    lives in the same building and has often come for
    supper, taken the sons north to fish, and been called in

professionally. Shorter than Walter—about five foot nine—he is gray-haired and wears glasses. His profession and life have taught him patience and irony. Lonely, he reads a good deal and has a cottage on the Cape and a garden to which he looks forward to retiring. Born in upstate New York, the Doctor has lost most of that region's odd twang but kept its dry, unhurried tone and pace.

MARION is thirty-five years old, very attractive, perhaps a bit heavy. She carries her weight well, though, and, in fact, it suits her. She describes one of her two failed marriages—her first—briefly in the course of the play. Her second ended four years ago. Shortly after the divorce, this second husband went off to Japan to represent his firm there and he has since married a docile Japanese girl with whom he can at least act out a marriage. He writes Marion occasionally to tell her how happy he is now, etc., and sends her expensive presents each Christmas to ensure getting at least a note. Like Walter, Marion was born in the Midwest. In Indiana. Her pudgy, apple-cheeked, Presbyterian-Republican father is still wringing Calvinist hands at the kind of life he excitedly imagines her to be leading. Poor Dad! In his sunset and autumnal years, when the fruits and dividends of life should be ripe for delectation, he finds them soured after each trip East where, in recent years, he has braced himself to meet, in Marion's apartment, a sinister procession of different men including two, admittedly, very genial Jews and a furious, clip-speeched Negro dressed up like some African. His daughter. Lord, why did she ever leave the Midwest, why did she ever leave home, why did she ever leave *him*? He blushes when he kisses her.

Dad has never met Walter, of course—though of all her men, he would find him most acceptable—a judgment his daughter feels seeping up through her own skin. What pleasure, though partly ironic, it would give Marion to say, introducing her third husband, "Dad. *This* is Walter." Between and after marriages, Marion has done the usual makeshift things: sold silverware from house to house (two days), been a receptionist, graced Schrafft's as a hostess, acted in summer-stock theaters (she thought she had a career there for a time) when there were parts that allowed her to play herself and when still another young director had fallen madly in love with her. She has also taught difficult children. Her present occupation is running a small jewelry shop. Some of the funds needed to set this venture up were obtained in a peculiar way. During the divorce proceedings with number two, Marion didn't demand a cent from her husband and, of course, wasn't legally entitled to. She had walked out on him and had offered enough evidence of her adulteries to satisfy the most pedantic judge. Her complete indifference to cash at that time, though, had confused her husband. He felt bad enough about not having been able to father a child on her. (She had badly wanted children.) He had felt even worse about the lack of a real blow-up at the end. She had sailed out too fast and much too casually for his taste. Was he *that* insignificant? So, to salve his conscience and to bring their relationship back to a point where he could feel at least financially in command, he had sent her a check—in lieu of alimony!—for $7,500. She did not, as he had half hoped, indignantly return his gift, but simply banked it. Marion, who can be pretty tough on occasion, is also the confused soul of hope—she goes on, she hasn't stiffened under her strains, she expects fulfillment at last. Her body tells her things her mind can't. Not intellectually bright, she is emotionally pretty wise and physically she has never been stingy.

EDWARD is twenty. He is thin and taller than the Doctor. He is fairly good looking; his voice is rather deep. Though his father frequently insists on Edward's close resemblance to his mother, the fact is that Edward's bone structure is similar, on a reduced scale, to his father's. Since he admires his father, Edward tries to carry himself as his father does and has also taken over some of his father's brusque gestures. Basically, Edward is not quite as gentle and almost overly sincere as he may seem to be out of shyness or fear; like his father, he is also subject to flashes of temper which reveal a substantial core that is hot and that won't take too much shoving around for too long. If he seems a bit stiff in this play, remember (among other things) that he is seen here only among adults and is trying to compete with adults. Edward stutters occasionally. For two reasons: one is that, when touching on the subject of his mother and her death, too many conflicting thoughts arise at once; the other is that a professor highly regarded at his college stutters and a number of his brighter students have picked this habit up—a kind of intellectual badge. Thus, he is sometimes more confident than one might think when he stutters. It gives him a personality—though one whose origin neither Marion nor Walter is acquainted with. Edward's love life, touched on occasionally in the play, has been as romantically disappointing as he could wish. He has always prudently picked girls to whom he could attach himself without incurring the threat of an overwhelmingly complete response. His girls have been good girls, fey girls, idealistic girls—girls, in short, who haven't yet found the bad man who will liberate them from their circle of self-enchantment. One of Edward's closest "friends" is his cousin Cynthia. Cynthia, who does not appear in the play, is the adopted daughter of the dead Louisa's sister Elaine and Elaine's "Command Generation" husband, Howard—the vehement old Boy Scout who is an editor of a weekly news magazine which admires tame Negroes and belligerently ignorant Republicans of the Nixon stripe. Last summer, there was an odd scene between Edward and Cynthia. They had been friends for so long; they had, at their different colleges, both suffered under the grave load of their chastity; and they had, at a distance, both nursed vague hopes of a breakthrough with each other. Furthermore, at the time of the scene, they were both warm and wet and wearing bathing suits. But Cynthia, who had had to defend her honor in college more than once, had developed a little ploy which, when the chips were down (to use her father's lingo), she used on Edward too. "Would you be very angry with me if I said I think we should wait?" And Edward, the fool, had looked at her fond eyes and said No, he wouldn't be angry. At which she blew up, saying he was just like all the rest of them, that they all said they wouldn't get angry and, if they really cared, they would! And would either take her right there or leave her. After which they had talked and talked and walked home hand in hand, still chaste, seething with chastity. So Edward still goes around, as his father says *he* did at that age, with a voice like a bullfrog and a bursting fly. Not quite a bullfrog, though. Just a rather deep voice.

NOTES ON THE STAGE

The staging of this play—and to some degree the writing of it—owes a good deal to Peter Zadek's production of Wedekind's *Frühlings Erwachen*. Zadek's use of sliding panels (only one was movable in his production) stripped the stage down to essentials. A large panel—bearing a significant big picture or design and covering about a third of the stage area—would slide to one side and reveal, in the area opened up, a bed and perhaps one chair; or a roof, a wall, and a window; or a desk; or simply space. You saw as much of a setting as was needed to suggest the scene and no more. At the close of a scene, the panel slid back, opening up another area with its sketched-in set. Thus, there were no halts in the action. Not only was the action speeded up to its proper tempo—or rather, for once, allowed to flow unimpeded—but words took on their full weight. Without any stunning *coup d'oeil* displays to applaud, without any naturalistic rubbish to stumble around or get lost in, the audience attended more carefully than usual. It had no choice in the matter. Called upon to contribute details, to imagine, to follow fast-moving action, the audience was roused from its traditional lethargy. (The production I saw was done in Holland.)

Still, when I first saw the production, my impression was that Zadek's staging was a kind of drastic (and very successful) restoring-technique. Confronted with a somewhat dated piece, he removed everything that, theatrically, dated it—except of course the fitting costumes, the significant props, and the urgent preoccupations of the author. These last, moreover, took on new life by being so freshly considered and simply framed. And by being very well acted—by the Haagsche Comedie. Acting on a stripped stage, the actors seemed liberated.

But Zadek's staging offers more than a means of restoring period pieces to new life. It shows how the stage may be used—within an apparently traditional framework—with the freedom of a film director using a camera. Transitions can be made as fast as cuts. Action can be anywhere, yet the where is defined. Action can flow.

It had other advantages—in working out my own play. This play is a memory lived through and, as such, it must be able to overshoot time lines as well as to reveal, in its pace, the mind of the man remembering the action. Furthermore, the play is meant to *seem* realistic only within severe limitations. It is meant to be acted as if played out again in a man's mind, not as if lived through for the first time. The setting—as I see it—lends itself to, and may even lead the audience to expect, this sort of playing. Though there is a degree of natural detail, those details are clearly subordinated to a style that shows a brusque disregard for naturalism.

In my play, two panels are used. Both can be moved. The stage-right panel, which covers about a third of the stage, is covered from top to bottom by a blown-up photograph of Manhattan. Resting on tracks on the stage floor (a bit downstage), the panel rises to the top of the stage. The photograph I have in mind is the famous Feininger picture showing the city rising up over the sloped shoulders of foreground tombstones. The stage-left panel is dominated by a photograph or painting of Walter's dead wife Louisa. Set in an oval frame, this picture takes up at least one third of the panel—the top third. Louisa's face is rather thin; there is hope in her eyes and a small smile on her lips. The picture includes her bust. A lovely woman. This may be enough for this panel, though it might be useful to include a picture of Walter's absent elder son Jim standing by the shining body of his jet fighter. If a director feels he can do with less realism on this panel, fine. But a picture of Louisa should follow the action with its eyes from some point stage left. The director is also invited to ignore almost all the light cues given here— they are only given to suggest the mood of certain scenes. Except for the beginning and end, when Walter should be isolated—a light figure alone in the darkness—a good strong surgically white light might well be kept on the stage throughout. This is, after all, an Anglo-Saxon chronicle.

The back wall of the stage is white-washed brick, from one side to the other.

Actors generally make entrances from behind panels and exit behind panels—not from stage right or left.

In the area in front of the panels there may be two low black cubes—for sitting. Furniture used behind the panels to set scenes appears, within one or another of the three areas (stage right, left, or center) as close, downstage, to the panel track as possible. Action starting behind a panel track may soon move out.

The furniture used in the center area remains the same from start to finish: a black leather, perhaps crescent-shaped, couch a bit right of center and a black leather chair, left.

NOTE: The sound of a jet passing over the city—a far up and off sound—may be heard infrequently.

A light comes up on WALTER, *standing mid-stage, alone. After a moment, he speaks.*

WALTER: Often, for instance, it starts like this:
    my in-laws—thank God—have just left,
    my friend the doctor is staying behind
    as relieved as I am, I trust,
    to be able to talk now they're gone,
    and I start to live through it all once again—
    hoping the end will be different.

    That picture there is all that's left of my wife.

    Now, as I say, my relations are gone.
    I can turn to the doctor and speak freely.

Light comes up in the center area. The DOCTOR *is there. Both men move now as if breaking into life.*

    Lord, what a waste of time it is to be related! Every time I see off my in-laws I wonder what did I do to deserve them? Him anyway. I suppose they came to console me in my hour of need once again?

DOCTOR: I suppose so, Walter.

WALTER: But they never mention her once!

DOCTOR: When you're out of the room they do.

WALTER: When I'm out of the room. Exactly. But when I'm around—not once. They steer clear of her, they steer clear of death as if it would bite them and yet isn't that what they came to . . . ?

> Yes, well. The only real consolation I get from that pack is looking at Elaine's fine shoulders and other accoutrements. How my dear brother-in-law does bore her. Actually, I wouldn't mind boring her myself from time to time. Would you, Doc?

DOCTOR: She is handsome.

WALTER: She is, as you say, handsome.

DOCTOR: Though not as handsome as Louisa was.

WALTER: Louisa.

DOCTOR: Yes.

WALTER: Well at least you mention her name. A relief! I mean, after all, she was a woman, she is dead, she did have a name—and all those people—her relatives, mine—they all just tiptoe around it. You'd think it was dirty. You'd think they had wiped it right out of their brains.

DOCTOR: They haven't though. They remember.

WALTER: Then why can't they remember out loud? I don't know. It's just that after an evening like that all I can feel is how terribly fake death makes most people behave. What—I'm curious, Doc—but seeing as many people die as you do in your job—what effect has it had on you anyway?

DOCTOR: What effect? Oh, some indifference, I suppose, on the one hand. On the other, it still makes me want to keep people alive—alive and healthy.

WALTER: Yes. But I mean on you personally. In your own life.

DOCTOR: Well, what else can it do? It intensifies my appetite for living, I guess—what appetite I have left.

WALTER: Exactly. Intensifies. Which is just what I can't
stand in that pussyfoot pack of . . . All death ever
does to them, as far as I can see, is make them a bit
more scared, a bit more uncomfortable, a bit more
boring. I mean I suppose it might have been different
if Louisa had suffered for months. But a crash like
that—one minute you're there; the next, crushed, on
fire and . . . All I can feel now is—you're alive, so live.

DOCTOR: Or you're dying. So live.

WALTER: Either way. But can you imagine—even now,
three months after it all . . . to still feel obliged to
look as glum, as washed out, as you possibly can?

DOCTOR: That wasn't . . . that wasn't quite the impression
you made this evening, Walter. (*The two men ex-
change an amused glance.*) I know what you mean,
though. Yes. The decent thing would be to apologize
for still being around in one piece.

WALTER: In one piece. Yes. That's bad enough. But to still
be around in one piece that's . . .

May one still speak frankly in this half-assed
world? At least to an old friend?

DOCTOR: Well, one may try.

WALTER: If I don't, I'll burst. What makes it urgent is . . .
Edward coming back tonight. You know how attached
he was to . . . to his mother. The trouble is I don't
quite know how to go about it. With him. With you
either, old sport.

Doctor, I suffer from an acute, middle-aged, and
inexcusable malady. I'm . . . Guess, Doctor. I'm a
living symptom.

DOCTOR: You're in love?

WALTER: You're an excellent doctor, Doctor.
Is there a cure?

DOCTOR: Only one, I'm afraid. You know that.

WALTER: To live it out?

DOCTOR: To see it through—yes.

WALTER: Yes.
Are you ashamed of me, Doctor?

DOCTOR: No.

WALTER: No?

DOCTOR: No. Why? Are you ashamed of yourself?

WALTER: I should be. I should be shocked. And some-times . . . sometimes I actually am. She's so much younger than I am.

DOCTOR: Does that really make any difference?

WALTER: Difference? I'll tell the world it does! Her youth brings out the youth in me. We make love like giants.
You're smiling, Doctor.

DOCTOR: It's only that . . . well, I guess I'm not used to hearing a man your age talk about . . . about that without immediately asking, in fear and trembling, what it will do to his heart.

WALTER: Oh, my heart. May it burst in bed.
I would like you to meet her.

DOCTOR: I would very much like to meet her. Her. She has . . . I trust she has a name.

WALTER: Yes.

DOCTOR: I see.

WALTER: What do you see, Doc?

DOCTOR: Nothing.

WALTER: I must . . . funny . . . I feel superstitious about some things, I guess. It's just that I don't want to let go of her name until you actually . . . lay eyes on her, as they say.
You really want to meet her?

DOCTOR: Of course.

WALTER: Well then, you shall. I'll ask her to come down.

DOCTOR: You mean she's here?

WALTER: Do you think I could have plowed through this evening if she hadn't been?

DOCTOR: I see.

WALTER: Yes? What?

DOCTOR: You really are suffering.

WALTER: Well I told you I was.

I held you out, Doctor, as one among other rewards for her patience.

DOCTOR: I'm honored. Genuinely.

WALTER: But?

DOCTOR: Well, don't be offended, Walter, but . . . you're really thinking of marrying then?

WALTER: You mean you wouldn't care to meet her if I weren't?

DOCTOR: Not at all. I'm just . . .

WALTER: Just what? Surprised?

DOCTOR: Well yes, a bi . . .

WALTER: Surprised? Or shocked.

DOCTOR: Look, Walter, don't try to bully me into saying things I'm not about to say. I *am* a bit surprised, yes. Hell. Aren't you?

WALTER: Nice to see you fight back for once, Doc.

DOCTOR: Just answer the question. You're as surprised as I am, aren't you?

WALTER: More.

I could hardly believe it. It all happened very fast. Now it can't go fast enough. I wish we had married last week. Yesterday. This morning.

Edward was very close to his mother. It will not be easy.

DOCTOR: And Jim?

WALTER: Jim? No. There's no problem there. I wrote him about it. Wrote him at length. Even sent him her picture. You know what he did? Taped it up in his cockpit. She's so young the wise bastards out there think it's *his* girl. Actually, she's not all that young. Thirty-five.

DOCTOR: Forty-eight.

WALTER: Thirteen. Yes. I know. So what?

DOCTOR: Exactly.

WALTER: Thirteen years' difference. Still, I figure two failed marriages on her side of the ledger must have aged her a bit, don't you?

DOCTOR: Two?

WALTER: Two.

DOCTOR: I don't know. Sometimes just one can do it if it goes on long enough.

WALTER: What?

Anyway, years aren't what count. After all, Louisa and I were the same age. Born in the same month, in fact. Our sign, the Scales. Edward's too. My God, every time I think of it . . . Can you imagine having to explain to a college boy that you're in love?

DOCTOR: If he were my own son, perhaps I . . .

WALTER: And what's worse, a college boy who . . . you know. It's not just that he's got Louisa's eyes, he's got that same . . . that same Quakerly tenderness which can be so sweet, so accepting, so terribly tolerant you want to behave your worst sometimes just to give it a real workout.

DOCTOR: I had forgotten Louisa was a Quaker.

WALTER: You forgot correctly then. Her distinguished forefathers were. But money corrupts, Doctor. By the time Louisa was born they had all turned proper—

Episcopalian. No, all she kept of her Friendly past was the "thee" and the "thy," and the "thine."

DOCTOR: Yes, I always liked that.

WALTER: Yes, it can be very sweet, very touching at times. You mean she used it on *you?*

DOCTOR: Occasionally.

WALTER: Really? I see.

DOCTOR: What do you see?

WALTER: It simply never entered my mind before. Well! You were fond of her?

DOCTOR: We were good friends—kindred spirits, as they used to say. But I'm not you, Walter, so don't suspect the worst.

WALTER: What do you mean, the . . . ? Oh. I . . . No, it's just that I'd always imagined it was *my* companionship, or mine and Jim's anyway, that brought you in so often. Well, one learns. Always too late, but one learns.

"Thee" and "thy." And I didn't notice a thing!

DOCTOR: It was only a friendship, Walter.

WALTER: Well of course it was.

On second thought—perhaps I'd better not ask you to meet . . . meet her tonight. No. It was just that, frankly, I did want her to meet somebody, a friend, before seeing Edward.

DOCTOR: You mean they're going to meet tonight?

WALTER: Well . . .

DOCTOR: You mean as soon as he gets home you're going to . . . ?

WALTER: Well don't blame me! Christ! I certainly hadn't planned it that way! As you know, he was expected back the day before yesterday. What was I supposed to do this evening when he called to say he had taken the bus instead of flying and would be getting in soon—excuse myself, rush out of the room, run upstairs and tell her to pack her little blue bag?

DOCTOR: Perhaps you should now.

WALTER: Why the hell should I, Doc? I'm not ashamed of her! I've been waiting to be with her. And Edward's got to meet her *some*time, doesn't he? Or am I supposed to give her up for the duration of young Mr. Edward's collegiate vacation? Is that what you want me to do?

DOCTOR: Do you want an answer or do you just want to shout?

WALTER: Both.

Excuse me.

What were you going to . . . ?

DOCTOR: I was thinking not so much of you as of her upstairs. And of Edward. I was thinking she might just possibly like to be prepared. I was also thinking that Edward too might like some time. People do appreciate knowing what to expect, you know. Or do you find that very old-fashioned now that you're suddenly so young again?

WALTER: Your bark is improving, Doctor. Do you ever bite?

DOCTOR: Do you?

WALTER: ————

DOCTOR: Well, with you one has to, at times.

WALTER: I appreciate it.

DOCTOR: I don't.

WALTER: No, you wouldn't. It's the latent martyr within thee, Doc.

DOCTOR: Call it whatever you like. I still think though that though you may enjoy ramming ahead, you might just stop to think how others may feel.

WALTER: A familiar phrase. My answer to that one used to be, But dear, if I keep stopping to think about that, when would I ever start anything?

Never.

Well, but you're right, of course. It just seemed easier to get it all over with before either of them had time to get all worked up. Anyway, what the hell! Edward can take it. He's not a child.

DOCTOR: Is he a man?

WALTER: Edward? A man? A good point. Still—as my pompous brother-in-law would say, He's got all the makings of a man.

Ass.

DOCTOR: It could be quite a shock.

WALTER: Meeting a beautiful woman usually is.

DOCTOR: No. I mean it.

WALTER: Well, and if he waits a week, if we talk a week, if I get worked up for a week and *then* he meets her?

I admit, though, if it hadn't worked out this way by itself, I would have preferred to . . . to lead up to it gradually. But if this is the way it's to be, so be it, I say.

DOCTOR: Then you're seriously thinking of marrying her?

WALTER: I don't know about seriously. I've been . . . I've been serious for years. But passionately—in hot flashes —yes, Doc. I am.

DOCTOR: And she?

WALTER: She's more prudent. She's been burned. It was she, for instance, who insisted on meeting Edward before we . . . Even after we'd heard from Jim. Insisted on waiting. Waiting? What for, I'd like to know. For our blood to cool off?

DOCTOR: No. For time.

WALTER: And—pray—what will time do, Doctor? Heal all wounds?

DOCTOR: To some degree, yes.

But more than that, what it often does, what it can do, is simply allow you to live out Louisa's death. I don't know how else to put it. I've seen it. The dead we have loved, and hated, live on in us for a long time—sometimes forever. And to thrive, we need their blessing.

WALTER: Their blessing.

Yes.

If I could only believe . . .

I don't know. Two days ago, though, when I expected Edward back, I went, for the first time since the funeral, into Louisa's room. Everything left as it was. A lovely room, full of light. And everything in its place. But on top of her writing desk, sealed and addressed and stamped, I found a letter addressed to Edward. There it was. Had been all that time, I suppose, if not longer. And I picked it up and I even held it up to the light to see if I could see through the envelope and read what it said. I couldn't see through. I couldn't make out a word and though I wanted to open it then and there and read it, I didn't. Instead, I put it away in a pocket to save for Edward's return. It's here now. And that unsent letter . . . Was she, I wonder, only writing the little news and much love she sent every week or was there news she could no longer share with me? I wonder. We need—as you say—their blessing.

DOCTOR: Good night.

WALTER: Good night.

The DOCTOR, *after a pause, starts off upstage right behind the panel.* WALTER *stands still. As the light in the center area fades, the stage-left panel slides right, closing the center area off. A dim blue light in the left area. An open bed, its sheets and blankets flung back, stands right just behind the panel track. To the left of the bed, a cushioned stool and a dressing table with its triptych of mirrors.* MARION, *combing her hair, sits on the stool. She is talking toward the mirrors in which she can—though the audience as yet cannot—see* WALTER. *Marion's hair is long and brown. She is agitated—angry but in high spirits. Though she is dressed, the back of her dress has not been zipped up yet. She has her stockings on but her shoes lie kicked off by the bed.*

MARION: Jesus, won't you ever grow up? I thought I was dumb but, boy, you beat anything I ever saw. Who do you think you are anyway? King Kong? No, I mean really, can't you ever think of anybody else or aren't we worthy of the big man's attention. Huh? If you ask me, you've been boss just a little too long for your own good and everybody else's too. Somebody ought to fire you fast.

Oh don't just grin. I'm not kidding. I'm furious, Walter. He could have walked in the house any minute, walked right in on us. He still could. Is that the way you want me to meet him? Is that all you care about me, about him? Don't you give a shit about anything? Well don't just snigger. Answer me.

Walter?

WALTER (*not yet on stage*): My dear?
MARION: Well?

WALTER *enters from behind the head of the bed, right. He is still buttoning his shirt, his cuffs are open, his feet bare.*

WALTER: I care. If I care more about being with you than seeing a son who isn't here anyway, forgive me.

MARION: Jeesus.

WALTER: Well, first things first. Will that do?

MARION: —————

WALTER: Second things second then. Is that any better?

MARION: —————

WALTER: I mean, Edward is a very nice boy but he is not quite what I would call a first thing. About fourth, I should say. Still out of sight while we're already home. A bit out of breath, I admit.

MARION *is applying make up, or facial creams, etc., with rapid strokes. Later, more slowly, she works on her eyes. No props needed.*

MARION: A bit out of breath. I'll say. Thanks to you and that hatful of rabbits you . . .

WALTER: Yes?

MARION: You really love getting into this kind of fix, don't you?

WALTER: Love it? No. But after putting up—for two solid hours—with that gang downstairs I was not, I assure you, going to let anything stand between me and my reward. Not even my son—also a relative, come to think of it.

Forgive me.

MARION (*rising*): Oh, forgive yourself. Just zip me up, will you please?

WALTER: I'm not sure I will.

MARION (*wedging her feet into her shoes*): Okay. Don't.

WALTER: All right then, I will. If you will kindly hold still, that is. (*He zips up the back of Marion's dress.*) You can relax, by the way. The call was from Newark.

MARION: I beg your pardon.

WALTER: Edward's call was from . . . Well, we were falling asleep. I had to wake us up somehow, didn't I?

MARION *regards* WALTER *with weary affection for a moment. Then she sits down by the dressing table.*

MARION: You know, Walter, I like this room and I like the view and sometimes I even like you but there're times I look in this mirror I wish your face wasn't anywhere in it. You know what I think? Sometimes I think that somewhere far back in the back of your head there's a little boy who's one of the meanest little boys I ever met in a man over forty. Don't you get awfully tired of him sometimes?

WALTER: My dear, I was for so long exactly my age and older . . . If I've turned into a boy, it's your fault. You've made me so young I forget myself sometimes and find myself back in knee pants, and behaving accordingly. Tomorrow—I promise you—I shall help an old lady across a busy street and try to square my account with heaven.

MARION: Wow. You really are odd, Walter. Lovely but odd.

WALTER: And you really are lovely, my dear. Lovely but lovely.

MARION: But he *is* coming?

WALTER: Yes.

MARION: I better clear out of here.

WALTER: I wish you wouldn't. I wish you would . . .

MARION: Look, Walter . . .

WALTER: I mean it.

MARION: Look. I'm not only a mess, I'm . . . I don't know *what* I am but one thing's for sure, I'm in no condition to . . .

WALTER: You're in perfect conditi . . .

MARION: . . . to meet anybody, much less your son.

WALTER: He's not an ogre, you know.

MARION: You know what I mean. Don't kid around. You know it's important.

WALTER: And I also know if we *make* it important, it will . . . All right. Fine. Yes. I'll . . . (*unspoken: calm down*) All I mean is, darling, if we put this little meeting off time and again, we will build it up into something very big, very emotional, very distressing, and very likely to be an extremely unpleasant family scene. That's why I thought that, if, just by chance, you two were to meet toni . . .

No. All right.

But there wouldn't be any need to mention our plans. Just, "this is *you*, this is Edward, how was your *trip*, let's have a . . ." No. I see. Wishful thinking?

MARION: I'll say.

WALTER: Yes. Still . . . I don't know how to say it.

MARION: ———

WALTER: I mean, if you are with me, I can . . . I feel I could love him, or at least accept him, and without you . . . I don't know. And I want very much to . . . to welcome him, to be gentle with him and not fall back into the way things have been in the past. Can't you see that?

MARION: I'll be with you. You know that.

WALTER: Yes, of course. But I mean physically there—next to me, or even on the other side of the room if you prefer. I need your help.

MARION: Walter, he's your son.

WALTER: My son.

MARION: Well he is!

WALTER: Did I say he wasn't?

MARION: No. You just sound so . . . What's wrong with him anyway?

WALTER: Nothing. He's a gem. An honest youth. A very clean-cut chap, as they used to say.

MARION: You mean he's a virgin?

WALTER: Exactly! At twenty. Mentally and physically a virgin!

MARION: Well, you were at that age. Remember?

WALTER: Good Christ, don't remind me. The good son with the bursting fly and a voice like a bullfrog. I should never have told you. A grotesque age! I can't stand to remember myself then and I can't stand to see it in him.

He won't understand a thing.

MARION: He'll understand. He just won't know.

WALTER: His mother's boy all right.

MARION: Yes?

WALTER: Right down to the color of his hair. His eyes.

That's what really gets me. Seeing her again. In him.

MARION: Walter . . .

WALTER: Especially after an evening like . . . The whole evening. They didn't mention her name. Not once.

MARION: Walter. I've got to go.

WALTER: Wait. Stay. Just a minute. Please. Imagine! A whole roomful of people—including her sister—and we talk about . . . It leaves me feeling, there she is, all locked up inside them, inside me, and if I could only talk about . . . I could be free of her for awhile. It's not always easy, holding her in. It's murder.

MARION: Tell me.

WALTER: You won't mind? It won't hurt?

MARION: It may. Tell me.

WALTER: People dream of being as close as we were once. It's a dream. Practically one person. Christ! A dream that becomes a nightmare when it's lived out as we lived it out in time. To have a person, to have a person joined to you that way—all your feelings felt, your thoughts thought, your moods shared. Until that person becomes more you than you are. Well, but do we love ourselves so much? Why—when she saw so much—why couldn't she see the one step farther to see how little patience I have with myself, that at times I can hardly bear myself? And how, later on, could she hope to share the me I needed to become for my work? A man has to harden and the woman who can't harden too is slowly but surely left behind— behind and bewildered. She stayed very soft, she stayed very gentle and, slowly but surely, I gave my own gentleness into her safe keeping. I left, as it were, one half of my life to her so that now, sometimes, I feel when I buried her I buried a part of myself. Dead, she works on me, touches me, moves me more strongly than she did in her last years alive. There are times—forgive me—but there are times when I touch you I can almost hear her say, "Yes. Do. Be happy. Live." It makes me cold all over, then doubly passionate. I drown out her voice in our passion. I finish her off. Yet when we're done, she returns. Very frail, but refreshed. How distant we were in those last years! Now that she's gone we are, at times, unbearably intimate. Though powerless as air, she frightens me. And Edward is her son.

Before I meet him, please—bless me. With the sign of the cross in kisses. With anything.

WALTER, *while speaking of his late wife, has perhaps been sitting either on the side of the bed or on the dressing-table stool, with* MARION *sitting on the floor in front of him, both facing out. There is a pause now.* WALTER *and* MARION *remain motionless as the stage-left panel slides left revealing, at the right edge of the center area,* EDWARD *standing. No suitcase, etc. The light in the center area comes up, and the light in the left area dims as soon as the panel starts moving.*

EDWARD: Father?
       Father?

WALTER *stands, fully dressed, stage left within the center area. He is looking straight ahead, but not at* EDWARD. *He holds an addressed, sealed air mail envelope lightly, by the tips of the fingers of both hands, as if weighing it.*

Father.

Both stand still on their opposite sides of the center area.

WALTER: Edward.
EDWARD: It's good to see you.
       What is it?
WALTER: I'm just looking. I'm sorry. Just . . . taking you in. (*Coming alert, he automatically puts the letter into his inside suitcoat pocket.*)
       You've changed.
EDWARD: Have I?
WALTER: Why yes. As a matter of fact, you have. You look —how should I put it—more like a man. I'm delighted.
       I don't suppose you *are* one, by any chance.
EDWARD: That depends on what you mean.

WALTER: How true.

Well. one thing's for sure—you're still a little prick, Edward. Christ, I send you money to fly with and what do you do? Bus your way cross-country.

I trust you're going to return the difference?

EDWARD: No.

WALTER: No?

EDWARD: No. In fact, I've already . . . I've already spent it.

WALTER: You what?

Don't tell me. I heard you. I just can't quite . . . Well, college at least seems to have given you a mind of your own.

EDWARD: Maybe it has.

WALTER: Not that I wouldn't have done exactly the same —if my father had been dumb enough or rich enough to throw that much money my way.

Good boy. Congratulations.

EDWARD: Thank you. I . . .

WALTER: Have a seat. You must be bushed.

EDWARD *sits*.

EDWARD: Any news?

WALTER: News? Oh, from Jim? Yes. A very relaxed letter. From Hong Kong of all places. Time's almost up over there. But you've heard from him, haven't you?

EDWARD: No. He hasn't written for . . . for at least a month. The last time I heard from him he was . . . he was thinking of signing up for another . . .

WALTER: Not any more he isn't.

EDWARD: No?

WALTER: No. I want that boy back here in one piece. In one piece alive, that is. Some wars may have been worth dying in. Not this one.

EDWARD: You really . . . ?

WALTER: Not this one by a long shot, though your brilliant editorial uncle-in-law defended our position over there most valiantly this evening—"a complex but crucial crusade" I believe he called it—while his lovely wife wilted on the sofa like the flower she is. To hear him talk, everybody over at his magazine is still playing dominoes—a game they learned from the Pentagon and just never outgrew, I guess.

EDWARD: Well, then you've changed too!

WALTER: What do you mean, I've changed?

EDWARD: You used to think it was a pretty good war, that we had a perfect right to . . .

WALTER: I did?

EDWARD: Darn right you did!

WALTER: Well, yes. Maybe I did. Before Jim got assigned to . . . Yes, perhaps I have changed.

EDWARD: I'm glad to hear it.

WALTER: Well, but so has *it*, don't forget that! There weren't half a million men over there once upon a time. The government wasn't addicted to lying once upon a time. And we weren't losing so many men over there once upon a time either!

EDWARD: Look! I couldn't agree with you more. I just said you'd changed, that's all!

WALTER: And you, sir, and what a relief, sir, have, as I said, got a mind of your own at last.

Still, there's no need to shout.

EDWARD: Sorry.

WALTER: Don't excuse yourself. As I said, it's a relief.

EDWARD: All right. Don't excuse me then.

WALTER: Don't worry. I won't.

You know, it's an odd thing. I was, frankly, **not** exactly not looking forward to your return but **not** quite sure either how we would get along with you back this time. It's a pleasure to see you, Edward.

EDWARD: It's a pleasure to see *you*, Father.

WALTER: Well, that takes care of that pleasure. Look, do we have anything else to say to each other or do you want to go up to bed?

EDWARD: You want to know . . . you want to know what I spent that money on?

WALTER: Why?

Don't tell me honest Edward has a confession to make?

You spent it on yourself, I trust?

EDWARD: No.

WALTER: You don't mean to tell me there's finally somebody in your life, as they say? Your acne's cleared up. I should have guessed.

EDWARD: No.

WALTER: No? Sorry to hear that.

Nobody?

EDWARD: Oh well, friends.

WALTER: Friends.

EDWARD: Very good friends, actually.

WALTER: Just that one never goes to bed with one's friends, does one?

EDWARD: ———

WALTER: So there's nobody.

Well why on earth not, Edward? I mean, it's the time, isn't it? You're all on your own. You're young. You used to run around with girls *here*. Christ! Jim had run through a whole sheik's harem by the time he was your . . .

Excuse me. I tend to forget. It wasn't part of my life then either. A failing I can never quite forgive myself.

EDWARD: How old were you?

WALTER: What?

I would be ashamed to tell you.

EDWARD: Tell me.

WALTER: Why on earth should I?

Oh, all right. But I'm warning you—if you smile in the wrong place, you're done for. I was twenty-four, Edward. Twenty-four years old. Four, five, six—oh, eight precious, irreplaceable years—lost. Don't—whatever you do—don't repeat my mistake. For my sake. For your own.

EDWARD: Then Mother was your first woman?

WALTER: ————————

EDWARD: I'm sorry. Please! We were just talking. It just came out. What can I say? I'm . . .

WALTER: Nothing. Forget it. She was. It's true. That's all there is to it.

So there's no one in your life?

EDWARD: They're all so . . . so idealistic. I think . . . sometimes I think they're so busy worrying about the world they forget they've got bodies.

WALTER: Remind them. Remind them, Edward. That, too, is a worthy ideal.

Well then, what *did* you lavish my money on if not women?

EDWARD: I wasn't going to tell you.

WALTER: What? Straightforward Edward? That's interesting.

EDWARD: I had . . . in fact I had a story all made up. I wasn't going to tell you, until you said what you did about the . . . the war.

I gave the money for relief . . . medical supplies, that kind of thing . . . for the North. I mean, I thought Jim has to do what he's doing against them and I

could do *some*thing, not against him but . . . for them.
After all, they're people too.

WALTER: I see.

EDWARD: And they're going through hell for something
they believe in more than we do in . . . Well, than
most people here do.

WALTER: A year ago I would have pounded your head in
for you. I would have, you know. Except that a year
ago your mother would have stopped me. Now what
can I say? I'm torn. Of course we can't call the South
a democracy but still, what do you do when a country's
existence is threatened like that? Walk out? Or are
we only supporting a clique, a clique and perhaps one
class of people? Your idiot uncle knows all the an-
swers but I . . . I simply don't know anymore. It's as
if—as she . . . as a friend, as somebody said the other
day—it's as if we're too big to hear anymore. Too big
and too rich and too scared to listen to any voice but
our own. Deaf somewhere. We can't hear anymore
and we're too proud to listen and we ram right ahead
and speak a whole different language, and we don't
have a clue.

Mind you, I'm not saying I agree with this person's opinion. Still, it's nice to surprise you. Or don't I?

EDWARD: I'll say you do.

WALTER: Well, even at my age a man *may* have interesting
friends, you know. I mean, much as it may astonish
you, even after college it does sometimes happen.
Maybe not quite so idealistic as your . . .

Yes.

Still, as far as sending relief to the North goes . . .
I trust you know those packages will never get there.

EDWARD: Probably not.

WALTER: No. That kind of stuff never does. Too innocent to survive.

At any rate, Edward, if your confession is over, consider yourself absolved.

And now, if you'll forgive me, I . . . I too have a confession to make.

EDWARD: You're . . . you're going into the priesthood?

WALTER: The . . . ?

Good Lord!

I keep forgetting you have a sense of humor, such as it is.

EDWARD: Well *you* don't have one. Somebody in the family has to.

WALTER: Perhaps I shouldn't have let you off so easy. You're not making things very easy for me, you know.

EDWARD: I know.

WALTER. Well, I wish you would.

EDWARD: Is it that hard to make?

WALTER: Yes.

EDWARD: You want to remarry?

WALTER: Who told you that? Jim tell you . . . ?

EDWARD: No!

WALTER: Then who . . . how could you possibly . . . ?

EDWARD: He didn't tell me in so many words but I could . . . And what other confession could you make anyway? That you were leaving your firm? You wouldn't!

WALTER: Are you done shouting now?

EDWARD: Yes.

WALTER: Well then, yes, I am planning to marry.

EDWARD: That's pretty fast, isn't it?

WALTER: I beg your pardon?

EDWARD: I said . . .

WALTER: I heard what you said. I'm not deaf, you know.

EDWARD: Three months. Jesus! Did you already know her?

WALTER: What?

EDWARD: Did you already know her before . . . ?

WALTER: Know her? What do you mean, "know her"? In the Biblical sense?

EDWARD: All right. In the Biblical sense.

WALTER: I didn't want it to be like this.

EDWARD: Well, this is the way it is.

WALTER: I did not want it to be like this. You haven't changed. I have. You haven't. You haven't grown up, you've just gotten cocky. You don't have a clue to what people mean to each other. Not a clue. Shut up. I'm talking.

What was I going to say?

(*To* MARION, *absent.*) Please.

EDWARD: I don't know *what* you were going to say. I just said it seemed pretty fast.

WALTER: It was. I was stunned. I thought . . . I was convinced I would never be happy again.

EDWARD: Well then . . . that's . . . I can understand that.

WALTER: You can?

EDWARD: Yes. But *did* you know her before?

WALTER: Is that so bloody important?

EDWARD: So you did.

WALTER: Know her? Yes. I knew her. I had seen her. We were . . .

EDWARD: Just friends?

WALTER: Yes! Friends!

EDWARD: All right. You were friends.

WALTER: You make it sound so dirty. Friends. A dirty word? Since when?

EDWARD: You made it sound dirty enough to me when I said I didn't sleep with them.

WALTER: I did not! I said no such thing.

Good Lord. Can't you talk without all this shouting?

EDWARD: Did Mother know about her?

WALTER: No. No. Why should she? What was there to say? "I have a good friend I want you to meet. She happens to be a woman"? There was nothing to confess. A friend. Is that such big news?

EDWARD: Apparently not.

WALTER: All right. Apparently not.

EDWARD: You don't think she felt it even?

WALTER: Oh Christ, Edward. Perhaps . . . perhaps, yes, she felt that indifference that infects ten out of every ten marriages at some point in life. Perhaps, yes, she felt I felt penned up, locked into our life for good. Perhaps she even . . .

But one lives through these things.

EDWARD: She didn't.

WALTER: What?

EDWARD: —————

WALTER: Well, am I to blame for that? What kind of hideous crack was that meant to be? Was I at the wheel? What are you driving at anyway?

EDWARD: I just said she did not live through the time you were talking about. That's all I said.

WALTER: I know. I'm sorry. It's been a . . . a long day, that's all. I need some air. I'm glad you're home. You must be exhausted. Go to bed. We'll have time tomorrow. We'll both be rested tomorrow. You must be exhausted. *I* am.

EDWARD: You really love her?

WALTER: Very much.

EDWARD: Can I meet her?

WALTER: Can you meet her? Of course! I'm very eager for you to . . . And she wants to meet you.

EDWARD: She does?

WALTER: Yes.

EDWARD: Well then. We will meet, won't we?

> *As the left panel slides right to cover the center area, dim lights come up downstage right and in the left area. A simplified bar rolls out from stage right in front of the panel. The bar: a foot rail, vertical supports which rise and split at the top to run horizontally, forming supports for the glass counter. The bar area is lit by a dim blue light. In the stage left area, the* DOCTOR *stands, perhaps by a street light. He wears a raincoat and carries an umbrella.* WALTER, *wearing a raincoat and unfurling an umbrella, enters the left area from behind the panel now covering the center area. The two men, after nodding to each other, cross right, leaning into the wind. Before entering the bar, they may look up at the city. Then they close their umbrellas, duck, and walk up to stand behind the bar. Canned music may be heard, playing softly. The two men hang their umbrellas from the bar.*

WALTER: No. No, in fact, compared to what I expected— not bad at all. He wants to meet her. All on his own, without any prompting, that's what the man said. Lord, the first time I saw her, I just stood there and gazed. At my age! I'm bushed.

DOCTOR: Let us drink. (*The* DOCTOR *nods to the bartender —who doesn't need to be seen—and puts up two fingers.*)

WALTER: Yes.

DOCTOR: An Irishman tried a riddle on me this morning.

WALTER: He did?

DOCTOR: "Can you tell me, Doctor, why there are so many bars in this city?"

WALTER: Yes.

DOCTOR: Well, can you?

WALTER: No.

DOCTOR: "To keep all the men in their cages."

WALTER: I see.

DOCTOR: He was suffering from cirrhosis himself, of course. You're grand company.

WALTER: I'm sorry.

The drinks have just been served. The DOCTOR *raises his glass. No props.*

DOCTOR: Well, here's to the peace which passeth.

WALTER: All understanding. Yes. (*They drink.*) Still, no matter how much we drink, we never quite get there. I don't, at any rate.

DOCTOR: It's always at the bottom of the next bottle.

WALTER: Is that why you drink so much more than you used to?

DOCTOR: Do I?

WALTER: You do indeed, Doctor. I've noted a marked progress over the years.

DOCTOR: Yes. Well. The nerve-ends get thirsty. No good for the trade, though. People aren't exactly reassured by the sight of a bottle when they visit a doctor. Not even the Irish. When I retire though, I shall dedicate myself to the three last things of this life—fishing, my garden, my books, and my bottle, and I'll get to the bottom at last.

WALTER: That's four.

DOCTOR: All right. Have it your own way. Four.

WALTER: You'll be glad to retire?

DOCTOR: Well, Walter, I think by my age I've looked into just about enough stomachs and throats. All I shall miss—and not too much either—is the people.

WALTER: You're fond of people?

DOCTOR: I confess . . . Yes. I am.

WALTER: Be a lawyer the next time around. It will cure you of that fondness in no time flat. A year at the most. Oh Lord, I have saved so much money for the rich.

DOCTOR: At least they pay well.

WALTER: Whatever made you become a doctor anyway, Doc?

DOCTOR: I thought I told you all about that once.

WALTER: Not me.

DOCTOR: My father was a farmer.

WALTER: Yes. Well, mine was a banker, until the Depression at least. Still, you know what I started out to be? A union lawyer. A real crusader. On the opposite side of the fence as far as I could get from my father—in those days. Now here I am up to my neck in corporate tax law.

DOCTOR: God moves in mysterious ways, His wonders to perform.

WALTER: Except there's nothing godly about my profession and, the Lord knows, nothing mysterious about . . . (*The* DOCTOR *nods right and raises fingers for two more drinks.*)

Just gradual. One choice after the other. First a choice of scholarships—West Coast or East. West for the unions, East for . . . And I chose East. Then a choice of friends, professors, courses, and then came the choice of a job—a job and a city. And then between women—between the ethereal Louisa or her more practical sister and, by the time I was married, there I was! I had apparently chosen and I was apparently me.

DOCTOR: Yes.

WALTER: Well, but, by George, I wasn't!

DOCTOR: You're passing understanding, friend.

WALTER: Well, don't you . . . ? No, you probably don't.

DOCTOR: Don't I what?

WALTER: I would love to laugh in their faces sometimes—laugh in their faces, tear up their money, spank their children, strip their wives, and punch hell out of all those servants they hire, like they hire us, to tiptoe around without saying a word but *smiling*. Smiling—Christ! The American disease if there ever was one. Our generals smile, even our assassins smile, and when I see a client I hate or a partner I can't stand, *I* smile!

You never feel that way about the people you have to . . . ? Whatever it is you do to them.

DOCTOR: Not really. No. I'd like to paint their bodies a different color sometimes. That's about as far as it goes. Preferably blue.

WALTER: Blue?

DOCTOR: Well, blue or orange.

WALTER: I find it hard to believe in people like you. Gentle to the core. That's why I bark at you. Just like I used to bark at Louisa, hoping to find, under all that gentleness, something vicious underneath. It would have been comforting. I never found it. She was not a fighter.

DOCTOR: No?

WALTER: Oh, maybe she was. At the start. But I won. Still, once you've won you've still got to live with them. The trouble is, pity isn't love by a long shot.

DOCTOR: Louisa spoke to me once about you.

WALTER: Yes?

DOCTOR: Yes.

WALTER: When?

DOCTOR: Oh three . . . four weeks, a month perhaps before she . . .

I'm drunk.

WALTER: What did she say?

DOCTOR: She called me "thee."

WALTER: What did she say?

DOCTOR: She said she was thinking of leaving you.

WALTER: ————

DOCTOR: Yes. We talked a long time. You were late getting back from the office. As usual. Should we perhaps . . . ? I could use some air.

"Should we perhaps leave?" A quick nod from WALTER, *who pulls an unseen bill from a pocket and lays it on the bar. The two men take their umbrellas and, as the canned music stops, go outside. The rain has stopped for a moment. They move downstage.*

She said she couldn't.

WALTER: Couldn't leave me?

DOCTOR: Yes.

WALTER: Why? The children?

DOCTOR: No. Because she still hoped.

WALTER: ————

DOCTOR: It was the time to make up her mind. Edward and Jim, both grown up, both out of the house. You working, overworked, bringing work home with you.

WALTER: It was a refuge! We had nothing to say.

DOCTOR: Of course it was. She knew that.

WALTER: Then why the hell didn't she blast me out of my chair? Why not just one good explosion? Just once?

DOCTOR: Perhaps because you had won too often before, Walter.

WALTER: Won. Won what?

DOCTOR: Whatever it is men win. I don't know.

WALTER: I don't either. But I kept right on winning, that's for sure, until there was nothing to win anymore.

The rain starts up again. The men open and raise their umbrellas.

Yet there was a time—I don't even remember when— a time I remember thinking: this hurts; who am I hurting? And I thought, soon, when the right time comes, I'll let up on her, I'll let up, we'll start all over. But the time never came, Doctor.

DOCTOR: No.

WALTER: The time never came.

DOCTOR: Well and I don't suppose it ever is only one time. More like . . . like you said yourself, your own list of choices that made you become . . . one by one. Except that Louisa ended in you. That was another reason she found it hard to just walk off, I suspect. Not just that she ended in you, but one by one she had dropped her friends for yours and finally the only ones left were yours. Even her sister—of course the husband's a bore—but even there you had built up a wall between them. And then the children were out of the house, as you say, and so were you, in a sense. Where else could she go?

WALTER: Anywhere. Nowhere. For a drive in the country. I must give Edward his letter.

DOCTOR: I wonder.

WALTER: Yes. And I wonder—what would have happened if you'd been younger, Doc, and less gentle.
Taxi! (*He hails a cab headed right.*)
Come on! Get a move on, Doc!

WALTER *runs—jumping a puddle—right. The* DOCTOR *stands still, then follows more slowly. The bar is rolled off right. Lights go off right and come up in the center area as the stage-left panel slides from center to left.* MARION *is sitting in the chair far left in the center area, looking out downstage. After a moment, she hears footsteps and rises, touches her hair and smooths her dress. Nobody enters. After a moment,* WALTER *enters from right from behind the right panel. No coat or umbrella. A flower in his buttonhole.*

WALTER: He'll be down in a minute. He was flat out. Sound asleep.

Darling. Please. Just relax.

All right then, don't. But he seems—really—quite eager, very pleased to meet you. Not resigned. Eager. (MARION *sits again.*)

My dear. You look so lovely . . . if only you wouldn't look so damn tense.

MARION: Just let me be tense, will you please? Just this once?

WALTER: All right.

MARION: Thank you.

I feel awful.

WALTER: Do you want me to tell him not to . . .

MARION: Oh just stop it, will you?

You know I want to go through with it but, hell, I have nerves. Don't you?

WALTER: Yes.

MARION: Well you look pretty calm to me. Pretty smug, in fact. You like seeing people suffer?

WALTER: I do not.

MARION: Then why look at me?

WALTER: I just happen to be very proud of you and very confident in you and also, as you may recall, it was you who insisted on this meeting before we . . .

MARION: I know.

WALTER: All right then.

And after all, please don't forget—he's only a boy.

MARION: You weren't so terribly calm about it all before you had to meet him, as I recall, Walter.

WALTER: No, I wasn't, was I?

MARION: No, you weren't.

WALTER: Well, I am now!

Oh for godsake, come off it. He's twenty. He's . . .

MARION: Oh for godsake, come off it yourself, Walter! Why can't you just let me be a mess for awhile instead of joking around as if it was the easiest thing in the world? Why can't you just let me alone and nervous instead of . . . ? Why can't you just let people be the way we are if that's the way we are instead of whipping everybody into shape for once, will you, Walt, for a change?

Oh now don't look hurt!

WALTER: I am not hurt.

MARION: No. You wouldn't be.

I'm sorry. (*She starts to cry.*)

WALTER: He's coming.

EDWARD *enters from the right, from behind the right panel.* MARION *pulls herself together. She rises.*

Marion. This is Edward.

EDWARD *looks at* MARION. *A quick intake of breath.* EDWARD *doesn't say anything.* MARION *looks at* EDWARD *and smiles a bit.* EDWARD *doesn't respond to her smile.*

He simply looks, as if quietly held by her, absorbed in her. WALTER *to* EDWARD:

Well?

MARION: Walter.

WALTER (*to* EDWARD): Well, aren't you going to say *any*th...?

MARION: Walter. Stop it.

WALTER: All right. All right. Let's all just observe a moment of silence, shall we, while son stares.

EDWARD: I just...

WALTER: Just what? Don't have any manners?

MARION: Walter.

EDWARD: I just woke up. And you're ... you're ... you're a very b ... beautiful woman.

WALTER: My apologies.

Well, what did you expect—a crone?

EDWARD *and* MARION *have stood their ground at a good distance from each other. They are relieved at the sight of each other.*

I seem to be in the way.

Aren't you two at least going to shake hands with each other?

Oh I give up. Good Lord. In my day people at least used to shake hands. Should I leave you two youngsters alone?

MARION: Would you?

WALTER: What?

MARION: I said would you?

WALTER: Are you serious?

MARION: Are you kidding—after the way you've been behaving?

Edward? What do you say? Should he leave us alone?

EDWARD: Well, it was . . . after all, it was his idea.

MARION: Good-bye, Walter.

Silence.

Oh, just for five minutes, darling. You deserve it.

WALTER: Five . . . ?

I see.

And can I trust you two to behave?

Don't . . . (*Unspoken:* . . . *answer that question.*)

All right. Five minutes then.

Well . . .

Good . . . good-bye.

WALTER *leaves the center area, going stage left behind the stage-left panel.*

MARION: Whew!

EDWARD: Con . . . congratulations.

MARION: I never thought we'd get away with it, did you? But, God, somebody had to stop him sometime. Right?

EDWARD: Right.

MARION: I hope you don't mind.

EDWARD: Mind? No. I . . . I've just n . . . never seen it done before. I didn't know it *could* be done. Nobody here ever tried it.

MARION: No?

EDWARD: Well Jim u . . . used to try. Nobody else had the nerve.

MARION: I'm not so sure I do either actually. Brrr.

EDWARD: I . . . I'm sorry. What did you say your name was again?

MARION: Marion.

EDWARD: Of course.

I'm not quite awake yet. It was a long trip.

MARION: Yes. It must have been.

EDWARD: Yes. It was.

MARION: Yes.

EDWARD: Where . . . where did you go to college, Marion?

MARION: I didn't.

EDWARD: I see. Well, sometimes I wish I didn't either.

MARION: Why?

EDWARD: Nothing applies.

MARION: Huh?

EDWARD: Nothing you learn applies anywhere. I mean, look at you. At least *you* know what to do.

MARION: I do? Like hell I do. I just make it up as I go along. I was crying before you came in.

EDWARD: You were?

MARION: You mean you couldn't tell? I thought I looked such a mess that's why you just stood there and . . .

EDWARD: Stared?

MARION: Yes.

EDWARD: No. That wasn't the reason.

How old are you?

MARION: God, you really lunge right in, don't you, Edward. I'm not as old as I feel, let's put it that way. I'm thirty-five actually.

EDWARD: I see.

MARION: You thought I was older?

EDWARD: No. Around thirty-five.

MARION: Well maybe you're right then after all, Edward —they don't teach you everything in college. You could have pretended I looked thirty, you know.

EDWARD: I'm sorry.

MARION: That's all right.

EDWARD: The only thing is, I guess, I wouldn't mind if

people thought I was older. I'd like to be older. I get awfully tired of being young sometimes. Did you?

MARION: When I used to be young, you mean? Christ, Edward, you must be as mixed up as I was awhile ago. You can't get anything out straight, can you?

Actually, it's a relief to meet somebody as screwed up as me for a change. One hell of a . . .

I swear too much. Do you?

EDWARD: No. Not enough. We were . . . or I was anyway . . . brought up to be pretty genteel. Pretty goddamn genteel. I was my . . . my mother's child.

MARION: Yes. I know.

EDWARD: He told you that?

MARION: Yes.

EDWARD: Well I didn't *want* to be but she sort of needed . . .

He may get caught up in saying "she sort of needed," repeat it carefully, then go on fluently.

. . . somebody and I was the one that was left.

MARION: I like you, Edward.

EDWARD: Yes. Well that was the way it was.

MARION: You did hear me, didn't you?

EDWARD: Yes.

MARION: Did your father tell you anything about me?

EDWARD: A little.

MARION: Did he tell you I've been married before?

EDWARD: No.

MARION: Twice.

EDWARD: Why do *you* tell me?

MARION: Huh? I don't know. To get it out of the way, I guess.

EDWARD: I see.

Do you have any children?

MARION: No.

EDWARD: Well, Jim will be coming back soon. You'll like him.

MARION: But I like *you*.

EDWARD: We're very different. Sometimes I think I'll never catch up.

MARION: You don't have to catch up with anybody, Edward. I mean, you're yourself.

EDWARD: Yes. Whatever that is. It . . . it isn't always enough though, is it.

MARION: What do you mean, it isn't e . . .
   You're right, though. No. It isn't. I wouldn't have cracked up so many marriages if it had been.
   The first time I was married, though, I was your age. Younger. Can you imagine?

EDWARD: No.

MARION: All I can say is, don't rush. There's plenty of time.

EDWARD: Father was twenty-four. That's pretty young too, don't you think?

MARION: Maybe. It depends.
   I mean it's a great age if everything works, if you're happy. And they were, I think. Don't you?

EDWARD: I guess so—then. M . . . Mother used to talk a lot about the old days. They didn't have much then.
   Do you think people are happier when they're poor?

MARION: Not on your life.

EDWARD: No. I guess not.

MARION: I bet you do though.

EDWARD: I just don't know!

MARION: Don't get me wrong. I don't mean they're any happier when they're rich. But being poor . . . don't kid yourself. It's no help to anybody for anything.

EDWARD: That's just what I mean. You know these things. I don't. Poor people don't get to college.

MARION: No.

EDWARD: And even if they did, you could count on me to learn too late whatever they had to tell me. Like, I was thinking about it on the bus for instance, you live with your parents for years and I must have been seventeen or even eighteen before I saw even a simple thing like that they weren't just parents but two people who'd been in love once. Eighteen years. Before that, they were just . . . you know, parents. You have to feel these things yourself before they . . . before they mean anything.

MARION: Yes.

EDWARD: Well—but by the time you're old enough to feel them, everything's changed!

MARION: I'm afraid you just left me behind, Edward. I'm a slow learner—remember?

EDWARD: No. All I mean is by the time I finally understood they really meant something to each other—then she started . . . she used to talk to me then sometimes about their life. I could tell it wasn't all that rosy. Just by the way she said it *was*, and what a wonderful man Father was—except when she said it there were tears in her eyes as if she had to remember a long way back how wonderful he was. That's all.

MARION: Yes.

EDWARD: But why couldn't she tell me it was all going wrong instead of making it all sound so good! He could be so cruel and there I was with this wonderful picture that didn't fit him at all! I wanted to hate his guts sometimes and then—there it was—I could tell there was something else, somebody I never saw, never really knew. Is it there?

MARION: Yes. It's there.

EDWARD: It is?

MARION: It's there. He can be very young, very naïve really, very quiet, and also very afraid of showing it.

EDWARD: Afraid of showing . . . I'll say. *She* couldn't live without it though. That's why she talked so much to me. That's why she needed me so much. *You* won't need me, will you?

MARION: I hope not that way, Edward.

EDWARD: Thank God.

And yet . . . she was a good mother. And maybe she *had* to be as soft as she was because he was so . . . *I* don't know. We were just getting to know each other and then—all of a sudden she was dead, that's all.

WALTER *enters.* EDWARD *gets up.* WALTER *is smiling, perhaps looking at his watch to prove his exile is up.*

Excuse . . . excuse me, Marion.

He leaves the center area, right behind the right panel. WALTER *stands still, left.* MARION *remains seated, looking after* EDWARD. *A silent moment or two.*

WALTER: What happened?
      He talked about Louisa?

MARION: ─────────

WALTER: It had to come out sometime.

MARION: ─────────

WALTER: But you got along?

MARION: We got along.

WALTER: Well that's a relief.

MARION: Yes.

WALTER: Well is he for us or against us?

MARION: He's for us.

WALTER: He is?

MARION: Yes.

WALTER: Thank God.

MARION: Yes. Thank God.

There's nobody against us now.

WALTER: Nobody *I* can think of.

MARION: Except you when you get in a rage like . . . Boy, was it ever nice to send you out of the room!

WALTER: I noticed you enjoyed it.

MARION: Well did you deserve it or didn't you?

WALTER: Perhaps I did. Now shall we just forget about . . .

MARION: Fine! If you'll just forget about how to behave that way. What gets into you anyway?

WALTER: ————

MARION: You were ready to smack him. Well, weren't you?

WALTER: How could I know what he was going to say— just standing there staring . . .

MARION: Well what's wrong with that? Is that a crime? To stare at a . . .

WALTER: Look. We are not a married couple yet so please don't behave as if we . . .

MARION: Not married! I'll say we're not. And one very good reason we're not is . . .

WALTER: Yes? I've been waiting for this. Is what?

MARION: You sometimes just scare me.

I don't like being scared.

I've been scared.

WALTER: I see.

MARION: I hope you do, Walter.

WALTER: It just seemed awfully rude to me, that's all. The first time you meet a woman, to stand there with your face hanging out.

MARION: I suppose it would. To a man.

WALTER: What? Oh. Yes.

MARION: I thought he had seen a ghost.

WALTER: You see what I mean?

MARION: That's still no reason to hit somebody!

WALTER: No! But then I didn't. Did I?

MARION: ―――――

WALTER: Look. You did beautifully. It may have been . . . it must have been a strain but now that it's over please don't take it all out on me.

MARION: Do you want him to hate you?

WALTER: What? No. Of course not. Why on earth . . .

MARION: He said he sometimes wanted to hate you but he couldn't.

WALTER: Of course he can't. After all . . .
Edward said that?

MARION: He's not as much like his mother as you think.

WALTER: No? Well, but then I'm not as much like his father as he thinks either, my dear. You've brought out a new man in me.

MARION: I wonder.
Do you really want to marry me?

WALTER: ―――――

MARION: You don't think the same thing will happen all over again?

WALTER: What are you talking about—the same thing. What thing?

MARION: Am I going to have to fight you all the time to keep you from going dead on me the way you did on . . .

WALTER: Stop it.

MARION: Why should I stop it? I need to know. I get tired of fighting sometimes. Why don't you fight yourself for a change? Why do you have to knock all the rest of us around? Do we all have to be like you to survive?

WALTER: Good Lord no!

MARION: Like hell we don't! I can feel it already in me. I

have to flare up every time you do or I start to feel
like . . .

WALTER: Yes.

MARION: Well, what's wrong? Can't you bear to be a bit
more . . . Well, just tender?

WALTER: Tender?

MARION: Yes. Tender.

WALTER: All right. And you'll earn our living? I'm sure you
could, you know. Of course you wouldn't remain a
woman very long. You would lose certain feelings
when you found they not only served no purpose in
your work but made it impossible to do what you're
doing, but you *could* earn a living.

MARION: I'm afraid I don't follow you.

WALTER: You don't think I know what I'm like sometimes? You don't think I feel it? You don't think I
know there's a whole slice of feelings I've learned to
do without simply to function—Good Lord, what a
word—to function day after . . . I assure you, darling,
I've got the tenderest little boy inside me you could
ever hope to lay eyes on and if I've learned one thing
in life it's that that boy is simply no help whatsoever.
He's the kind you fire after one week at work. The
kind *I* fire anyway. I have yet to see a single job in this
country, a job with a future as they say, in which that
sensitive, that tender young man could function effi-
ciently for as long as a day. Still, he does survive. And
the odd thing is as long as I'm fighting, I know he's
still there. I know because when I get very angry, very
excited, he just gets quieter and quieter until, inside,
you could hear a pin drop.

Listen.

You see how tender he is?

MARION: Except you weren't angry just now.

WALTER: No. And to tell the truth, I didn't even know he was there until you blew up at me. You see why I love fighting you? You teach me who I am.

MARION: You're a weird guy, Walter. I've known some weird people in my time but you . . . there's no two ways about it . . . you beat them all.

WALTER: Then might I suggest a truce?

MARION: Fine with me, Walter.

WALTER: Shall we shake on it?

WALTER extends his right hand. MARION takes it. They shake hands slowly and formally. Then WALTER kisses her hand formally; then he kisses her on each cheek.

I hereby formally declare a state of peace between us.

MARION: Aren't you going to pin a medal on my chest or something?

WALTER: I shall. Yes. At a special candlelight ceremony. It will be held tonight.

They are walking downstage slowly, hand in hand.

MARION: Really, General. And do you make love as well as you make war?

WALTER: Better. You may melt my sword into plowshares. It shall remain true steel. (*He stops, turns toward* MARION.)

You know—at this moment anyway—I feel extremely happy. For the first time in years. You are so good. You don't give in. You are so kind. I only wish you could be as confident in yourself as I am in you. I see much happiness ahead. And now that I've waited, with my customary patience, and you've met Edward and it went very well, I wonder—what else are we waiting for?

MARION: You gave him the letter?

WALTER: ⸺⸺⸺

MARION: Do.

> Though I still, Walter . . . just like me meeting Edward . . . I still think you're just building something small up into something big when it may not be at all. You say yourself she wrote them both every week. Why can't it just be a letter? Do you want *me* to open it? I will.

WALTER: No.

MARION: Well what can I do then?

WALTER: What?

MARION: Is there anything I can do?

WALTER: Would you give it to him?

MARION: Me? Why me?

WALTER: Because! Because I am simply afraid sometimes of what I might do if that letter is anything except, as you say, just a letter.

MARION: But why should it be? I don't get it. Nobody even mentioned it was . . . well, anything except an accident. Nobody even thought of it. What makes you think . . . ?

WALTER: I don't. Or if I think of it at all, it's only because there's the letter, left behind, for him.

MARION: And nothing happened . . . nothing special happened that day?

WALTER: Nothing at all. Just the usual things. I kissed her good-bye, she straightened my tie, I picked up my briefcase, I left. A routine we had gone through five days a week for years. No explosion. No quarrel. Nothing.

MARION: I see.

WALTER: In fact, the only unusual thing I can recall is the weather—a brilliant, clear, very fresh day. Everything looked new. Even the buildings.

You're right. I'm getting all worked up about . . .
It's just that having waited all this time now . . .
Though it's been only three days since I found it,
actually.

MARION: All right. But at my place then. Not here.

WALTER: What's wrong with . . . ? Yes. Fine. Whatever
you say.

You'll do it?

MARION: Well, one of us has to.

WALTER: When?

MARION: Look. Don't rush it, will you?

He could come over for . . . well, for drinks, I
suppose.

WALTER: No. I don't like that.

MARION: You'd prefer if I invited him over for tea?

WALTER: Tea? Yes.

MARION: I suppose you know what "tea" means to people
his age?

WALTER: What? Oh, no. Not to Edward, it doesn't. Edward's a decent lad. At least I hope he is.

So you want him all to yourself in your apartment,
do you?

MARION: Uh-huh.

WALTER: And I suppose you'll come to the door in your
black silk . . .

MARION: Uh-huh.

WALTER: With just a touch of perfume behind each ear
and the sound of the hot shower already running.

Oh my oh my. The lucky little prick.

What *will* you wear?

MARION: This.

WALTER: You think that's wise?

MARION: Well, if you don't like my clothes I could always
wear nothing, Walter.

WALTER: You could too. I wouldn't put anything past you after the life you've led. Thank God, Edward isn't a man yet.

MARION: No?

WALTER: Oh he is not. He told me himself.

MARION: Oh but he is, Walter. Take my word for it. And you will admit I know something about men.

WALTER: Thank you for reminding me.

MARION: Well which do you like, Walter? You laugh at Edward's innocence and you don't much care for my kind of experience which leaves what?

WALTER: Where'd all this blow up from?

MARION: I just wish you'd face up, that's all. I can just see you—in about two years—starting in on me the way you did on . . . the way you do on Edward. I mean, we've all got our problems, we're all full of holes. Or maybe you aren't.

WALTER: Easy.

MARION: Well sometimes you push people around as if you thought you were God.

WALTER: I think that's enough now.

MARION: Yes. Sometimes it scares me. That's all.

WALTER: You don't think it scares me?

MARION: Be gentle with him.

WALTER: Gentle? I'm doing what I can. I'm sending him over to you—remember?

MARION: So I can give him a letter.
          Yes. I remember.

As WALTER *brings the letter out of his pocket, the right panel slides left to cover the center area. In the right area: a low coffee table, two chairs.* EDWARD *is seated, right.* MARION *stands, left. On the table: a tea pot, cups, a sugar bowl.*

EDWARD: No. He just m . . . made it sound so mysterious, that's all—as if . . .

MARION: Yes?

EDWARD: I don't know. As if he didn't really like the idea but thought we should . . . well, get to know each other better, I guess.

MARION: Well what do *you* think? Should we?

EDWARD: Definitely.

MARION: Maybe I just wanted to see you awake for a change.

EDWARD: I'm awake all right.

MARION: And maybe it's a relief for me to talk to somebody my own . . . Jesus, what am I saying? My own age. But I *feel* we are. Don't you?

EDWARD: No.
   I mean yes—I do actually. Really. You're very young.

MARION: You're learning, Edward.

EDWARD: But I mean . . . (*Unspoken: it.*)

MARION: You're learning. We'll make a man out of you yet. Though you're *not* very good at lying, are you?

EDWARD: No. But I wasn't lying. You are young.

MARION: Sure. Young enough to be your mother—or step-mother anyway.
   Would you like that?

EDWARD: Very much.

MARION: Yes?

EDWARD: Yes.

MARION: So would I.

EDWARD: What's wrong?

MARION: I just worry sometimes.

EDWARD: About what?

MARION: Myself. People.
   You can still get worried about wars. Well, so can

I, but what really scares the hell out of me is . . . just people. Stay in college as long as you can, Eddie. It may not be real but it's safer than the outside by a long shot.

EDWARD: I've been safe long enough. Some . . . sometimes it seems to me all I've ever done is go to schools.

MARION: Well, at least you go to good ones.

EDWARD: Marvelous.

MARION: You know where I went? You should count your blessings.

EDWARD: Why? Where'd you go?

MARION: I went to one of those Mother Hubbard finishing schools that—brother—really lives up to its name. Boy, when I got out of there all I knew was that the Mississippi was a very long river and that the one thing in life was to get married fast. If you're ever hungry for a woman, Edward, just drop in on one of those joints. They're crawling up the walls for a man. On the other hand, forget about it. They check with the bank first and then put a ring through your nose before letting you get to first base. The bitches. Well, I was just as bitchy and dumb as the rest of them. Dumber. Then there I was married and where was I then? I was really finished. It lasted six months. I mean, really Edward, you may kick it but a good education might have helped me a lot. You should be glad you're learning. Just to have all that time to grow up.

EDWARD: Yes?

MARION: You're damn right you should.

EDWARD: All right. I'm glad. Is that better?

MARION: Jesus. You're as bad as your father.

EDWARD: It just seems so remote, that's all. I mean, everything. Sometimes when I cross the campus I wish they'd tear down that whole fancy complex—and that's just the right word for it, complex—I wish they'd tear down those buildings that cost a fortune to build and . . . I don't know . . . maybe hold classes on flatcars, trailers, anything. At least you could move around, see things. And, like the war too. We get all excited and we're miles away and there's Jim over there at least doing something even if he's not sure it's right anymore and there we sit in a complex of buildings and we're sure it's wrong but what can we do? Talk. Demonstrate. Send packages off that won't get anywhere anyway.

MARION: Yes. Walter told me about that.

EDWARD: Well, and he paid for those packages too, in a way. For everything. I mean, that's part of the whole trouble with college. You learn and learn and the more you learn the more you see what's wrong with the whole . . . the whole system and yet there he is, paying for it, and he's part of the system too!

MARION: Who? Walter? He's not part of any system I ever heard of.

EDWARD: He does what he does five days a week, doesn't he? It may not make him very happy but he's been doing it for years!

MARION: Well what do you want him to do, Edward—sell beads?

EDWARD: I don't know. All I see is . . . I mean all these . . . well, like friends of mine. They live off their fathers too and their fathers all use the same excuse: they do what they do for their wives, their families, that kind of thing, and we all rebel I guess until we have families, and then we get *our* jobs and so it just goes on and on. But you take a factory worker, a man on the assembly line, at least he doesn't pretend to *like* his job. It's the men above him who have to pretend. Father pretends, and I'll bet when he's at the office he really enjoys it too. He helps run it, he gets paid very well, he can shove people around—except for his clients, of course. But why don't they admit it's not the screwy kind of work they do but the power or the money they really like?

Have you ever *been* there?

MARION: Where?

EDWARD: At the office?

MARION: No.

EDWARD: Well it's a factory too. Except that everyone's very well educated, everyone's very well dressed, and yet all they do—Father says it himself—is figure out how to save money for people who already have more than enough. What *I* can't figure out is . . . I mean he's blunt enough at home, but can you imagine Father having to be friendly to people he can't stand the sight of? I think that's wu . . . one reason his temper's so short. He can't really blow up all day but he sure can at home all right.

I'm sorry.

MARION: No. It's true. I just never thought about it that way.

EDWARD: I mean I guess when you start out it's still pretty interesting—any business—but then you work your way up and wh . . . wh . . . where are you?

MARION: Yes.

EDWARD: You're at the top!

MARION: Yes.

EDWARD: I'm still at the bottom.

MARION: Maybe that's one reason we get along.

EDWARD: Because I'm at the bottom?

MARION: You don't think I am too?

EDWARD: You? No.

MARION: Well I am.

I have another chance now. To start up again. And if you think age helps any, you're crazy. All it does for me is, by now I'm almost afraid to get what I want because I'll break it. It's the kind of thing I can hardly talk to your father about. He's so sure of himself. He bowls right over me. Especially when I can hardly say what the trouble is. I can talk, with you. I can even think when I'm talking with you. You have to know where you are before you talk to your father. I mean, if he could only joke about it—say, "sure our marriage'll be a flop, but let's try anyway." But he can't imagine what it's like not to be confident. And he thinks I'm tough because I have to be, with him.

Do you think I'm tough?

EDWARD: No. Well . . .

MARION: No, well I'm not. I can get scared pretty easy.

I want it to work this time. You're one reason I do.

EDWARD: Yes. We get along, don't we?

MARION: "We get along." I'll say we do.

EDWARD: You know, I've never . . . never talked to a woman the way I can with you.

MARION: I'm glad.

EDWARD: In fact you're the only older person I kn . . .

MARION: Thank you.

EDWARD: No. I mean who doesn't rub it in that she knows more.

MARION: Funny. You'd never guess it now, Ed, but I wasn't at all looking forward to meeting you at first. Scared stiff, in fact. It was just the only way I could put your father off. And now, here we . . .

EDWARD: You mean he wanted to marry you right away after . . . ?

MARION: We had known each other for some time, Edward.

EDWARD: How long?

MARION: Nearly a year.

EDWARD: I see.

MARION: What do you see, Edward?

EDWARD: Why Mother wanted to die.

A pause.

MARION: She never knew, Edward.

EDWARD: How do you know she never knew?

MARION: She didn't. Believe me.

EDWARD: Like hell she didn't. She would.

MARION: She didn't.

EDWARD: That makes it all the worse. That makes it really . . .

MARION: Yes? But look at me when you say it.

EDWARD: Nothing. I don't understand these things. You're all so much . . . or he is.

MARION: Yes. We are older. When it comes to that.

Will you listen to me though for a minute if I try to . . .

Though, Lord, how can I explain anything to you when it turned out the way it . . .

I can't.

EDWARD: Explain it. Please.

MARION: We didn't think anything would come of it, that's all. We used to meet. We used to say, nothing would come of it. He didn't want a divorce. I sure as hell didn't want to get married. We were fond of each other. We thought we could help each other. We really believed in some weird things, Edward. I really believed I could wake him up and get him going again and his marriage would work again and, for once, I would have done something for somebody and could walk off feeling . . . well, feeling I hadn't smashed everything or been smashed for once. Walter too. I was really a mess when we met. Wild. I didn't care who I was with because what difference did it make? Walter took me in hand so fast I didn't have time to say boo. He slapped me around and pulled me together and with him—believe you me—you find out fast enough who you are. He lets you know who he is fast enough. And I came to know, with him. But he loved his . . . his sons. He didn't want it to last. So we would both help each other and then go our own ways. But we just kept getting closer and closer and it helps if you know it won't last and then all of a sudden she died.

EDWARD: Yes.

MARION: But do you get what I mean? We were just trying to help each other. There just wasn't enough between them then for him to live from.

EDWARD: Whose fault was that?

MARION: Whose fault? Who knows? Both. It always is.

EDWARD: He beat her down and then he left her there. That's why she needed me.

MARION: Okay. That's it then.

EDWARD: Well is it or isn't it?

MARION: I got beat pretty hard too, Edward. I walked right out.

EDWARD: You didn't have children.

MARION: Well, I can't answer that. No. I didn't have children. So a woman lives through . . . lives through a dead marriage for her children?

EDWARD: ————

MARION: Okay. But then don't laugh at men who go on doing the jobs they do, for their children. A dead marriage—a dead job—there's not much difference. Except maybe that men can harden and still be men— but a hard woman? I tell you, Edward, I just don't know whose fault.

EDWARD: Neither do I.

MARION: Do you want to?

EDWARD: I don't have much choice. I never will.

MARION: Maybe you will.

EDWARD: Yes?

MARION: Maybe.

I have a letter for you. From your mother. It never got sent. Walter found it. He asked me to give it to you. (*She puts the letter on the table.*)

EDWARD: Yes? Why? Why didn't he give it to me himself?

MARION: He was afraid.

EDWARD: Afraid? (*He picks up the letter and tears open one end of the envelope.*)

Of what?

MARION: Of not being able to . . . Of what he might do if . . . Read it.

EDWARD: But I don't understand. Are you afraid too?

MARION: Me? No. I can always just walk away. You can't. Read it.

EDWARD: But why should you leave? You mean, leave *us?*

MARION: If I have to. Yes. Read it.

EDWARD *unfolds the letter and looks at it. It is short. Then he looks at* MARION.

It wasn't an accident. She wanted to die. Didn't she?

EDWARD *crumples the letter up in one hand.*

EDWARD: No.
MARION: Tell me the truth, Edward.
EDWARD: No. She did not want to die.
MARION: So it's only a letter?
EDWARD: Only a letter. The usual news. Nothing.

A *pause*.

MARION: You're no longer a boy, are you, Edward?

A moment later, all the stage lights go out; then, quickly, white light in broad horizontal bands starts running across and up the right panel of the city while this panel still covers the center area. The lights begin to form into words which remain, however, unreadable as they streak up the panel. The right panel then begins to slide right. The increasingly legible words now slide away from it to play across a white panel which has been let down from the top just behind the two panels. This panel measures about six feet from bottom to top; it spans the center area. The effect now is of the news bulletin lights in Times Square; the rushing bands may be accompanied by a sort of soft swishing or crackling sound. At last, running in from the right and off to the left and back on again, the words spell out:

IN FIERCE HAND TO HAND COMBAT   V.C. LOSSES
HIGH   DEATH TOLL   354   U.S. LOSSES MODERATE
SIX U.S. PLANES DOWNED IN MASSIVE ATTACK ON
HAIPHONG

As the lights come up again, the words are still running their circuit, repeating themselves. They fade out as the white panel is raised up out of sight. EDWARD

*is seen sitting downstage left, his back to the audience.
He is looking up at the picture of his mother. Music
is playing—"Canción de cuna," from Five Centuries
of Spanish Song, sung by Victoria de los Angeles
(Victor Red Seal LM–2144).* WALTER *and the* DOCTOR
*enter the center area from right, from behind the
right panel. After a pause,* WALTER *speaks.*

WALTER: More men down and more to go. Six planes,
five planes, four planes, three. Then just one—the
one all your hopes are riding on. Christ! It's like some
bloody countdown to what? To death, that's all.
Thank God at their altitude they don't have to see
the faces below them turning to mush, but how many
times, I wonder, how many times can a man fly over
it all without being brought down to the same human
mush himself?

   To fly over it all and not even hear one voice,
one yell. That kind of silence—incredible.

   I refuse—I simply refuse to go on. It's as if, when
pain builds up to a certain point, I'd lived through
it all before and can see . . . The news. And the way
Edward came back just now. Comes back, walks right
past me hardly saying a word, goes to his room, sits
there . . . listening to music. Her music. We were
going to celebrate—all of us—when he came back.
No celebration now. Yet when I asked him about the
letter, he said, "No"; he said, "No, she did not kill
herself, Father"—and left me standing there let off
by his words but convicted in his eyes of . . . Sweet
Jesus! I feel like ripping his face off to get to what's
hidden inside it. Hatred, or pity for me now, I suppose. A hatred or pity that rots my new life before

it can even . . . New life. All I feel now is old pain, as if I had lived through this all before, just as I've heard that music before. Her music. Listen.

WALTER *and the* DOCTOR *listen to the music for a time. Then the song is over.*

Tell me, Doctor. Jim will never get home, alive in one piece, will he?

DOCTOR: No.

WALTER: He'll be brought down?

DOCTOR: He'll be brought down.

WALTER: And Edward? What will I do to him? Will I kill him, Doctor?

DOCTOR: You can't see it all then, can you?

WALTER: No.

DOCTOR: No. The things you can still change still have to be lived. And there *are* things you still can save.

WALTER: Marion?

DOCTOR: You *can*. Yes.

WALTER: And Edward too still can be saved?

DOCTOR: The things you could change will have to be lived. So we'll see.

WALTER: Then I shall try. I'll call him down.
    But, Doctor, one thing before I see Edward.
    It's odd, but I feel . . . I feel
    if for once I could feel, undergo, *his* pain
    instead of my own
    there might finally be some blessing—
    a blessing in death and on our lives.

DOCTOR: Then you must be Edward. And Edward, you.

As WALTER *and the* DOCTOR *have been talking,* EDWARD *has set fire to the letter and, holding it up, let it burn down to his fingers. Now* EDWARD *rises, walks center.*

WALTER *and* EDWARD *look at each other, shake hands,*
perhaps touch cheeks on both sides. Then EDWARD
stands center, WALTER *sits left. The* DOCTOR *walks—*
during their enactment of the following scene—down-
stage right.

The telegram has just come. Jim is dead.

EDWARD *looks at the telegram, then crumples it up,*
then turns slowly to look at WALTER *sitting.* EDWARD
falls to his knees and pounds his fists on the floor.
Then he looks at his fists. Then he rises and goes to
stand, facing down, near WALTER.

EDWARD: Your brother is dead.
I said, your brother is dead.
Have you nothing to say?
My son.

I only had one, you know.
Your mother had you.
My son is dead now
and you don't say a word.

Why him?
I can't understand it.
He knew how to live
while you—not a word;
just pity, perhaps, like your mother's
horrible pity for me.

Look at her eyes. They're yours.
The same pity and sadness and softness
as if I could not understand I
was killing myself in her.
I could, finally, not bear—
I could finally not stand

looking into those eyes
full of mourning.

Sweet Christ, yes, he was your brother too
but my son, who is dead now,
while here you sit—not a word—
stinking with pity.

Was it pity for Marion, pity for me
that made you lie in her face
saying No when the answer was . . .
What? Was your pure boy's heart
so deeply moved, for once you could lie
like a man without flinching?
About your mother's last words, at that!

And still not a word.
But you don't think I know
the truth of the matter?
Your mother was never careless.
The morning she left for her drive
there wasn't a cloud in the sky,
there wasn't a car on that small
country road she chose for its flowers
—its innocent beauty—
which must, for a moment,
have made her feel young,
the bride full of hope, for a moment.
It took only one swerve for her then
to be burning at last as brightly herself
as the flowers of heaven, and out.

And still you have nothing to say.
How silent my boy has become!
The Lord only knows why you don't
follow her shining example yourself and take

the easy way out that ruins only
everyone else's life, while out you go
pure as a star. Why not, boy—
one last grand package to nowhere?

But still not a word from this hero
whose manliest gesture in a time of war
is to worry his conscience to the breaking point
and then, at last—but I won't rub it in—
while down comes his brother, brought down
and down, wound in a sheet of fire.

Why can't you talk at least,
tell me at least that you hate me
for the joy I took in seeing my son,
your brother, live as I would have lived—
or for having driven your mother,
your too gentle mother to . . .
But no. You say I didn't.
You refuse, like the good boy you are,
to say any such thing. You say no
and burn all the evidence. The proof
is inside you now. The truth is inside you.
Well, out with it! Tell me the truth about me.
That I killed her slowly.
That I kill.
That I kill.
That I kill.

As he speaks these last three sentences, EDWARD
pounds WALTER—*on the back, shoulders, head. The
pounding is both savage and clearly stylized. The
rhythm of the punches, the groans* WALTER *lets out,
the sound effects—a drum perhaps for the punches—
all should make the acting-out clearly an "act."*

WALTER *crouches, his hands over his head, reeling with the blows. Then* EDWARD *kicks him once and steps back.*

Still not a word.
You could hear a pin drop.
(*Drily.*) I pity you, Edward.

EDWARD *then crosses into the center area.* WALTER *rises and goes left behind the left panel.* MARION *enters the center area from right, from behind the right panel. The* DOCTOR *moves upstage.*

MARION: What did you do to him?
EDWARD: Nothing.
MARION: What did you do?
EDWARD: My son is dead.
MARION: You killed him?
EDWARD: No. *My* son. My son is dead.

As both panels now slide off-stage, WALTER *is revealed —in the left area—sitting on the floor, facing downstage. Behind him, a long blown-up photograph of* EDWARD *sitting where* WALTER *sits hangs down to just above the floor. Its bottom edge is already smoking, on fire.* WALTER *holds a still burning match in one hand. The photograph suddenly blazes up fast to the top.* WALTER *blows out the match, then rises. As he moves downstage center—to his position at the start of the play—*EDWARD, MARION *and the* DOCTOR *move to form a row upstage center.* WALTER *stands still, under a vertical spot, as he speaks. The three behind him stand in a light which, as he speaks, slowly dims and goes out.*

WALTER: There are parts, as you see, I can't face.

Can't clearly recall even now.
I don't, for instance, remember
ever striking Edward at all.
I only remember seeing him lying,
a heap on the floor. It surprised me
to see him there, nor could I have seen
any connection between the two of us then—
me standing, him lying—if I hadn't felt
a pain in my hands as if I had broken
a finger, or a bone in my finger.
Yet I swear I do not recall
having so much as touched him
so great was the distance between anger and me,
as great as the difference between
my voice and a silence inside me
as mute as a god.

There's no one to ask how it all
happened now. The doctor has left
the exploding city for a neck of the woods
I would not feel at home in and have not
been invited to either. Marion vanished
with a look on her face I recall
having seen before. And my sons—
they have gone too their various ways
leaving the ashes of wrath and compassion
for me to sift by myself.
And I would study compassion
if it weren't that it led me to see,
within the face of each person, my own—
a face I have reason to fear.

Thus I'm alone,
left alone to remember, to start at some point

and remember again
what it was like,
what it was like to be living
still bound to a woman,
still connected with men.

END